ONE-POT KETO COOKING

75
Delicious Low-Carb Meals
for the Busy Cook

CHARLOTTE SMYTHE

**CREATOR OF
CLEAN FOODIE CRAVINGS**

PAGE STREET
PUBLISHING CO.

PAGE STREET
PUBLISHING CO.

First published in 2020 by

Page Street Publishing Co.

27 Congress Street, Suite 105

Salem, MA 01970

www.pagestreetpublishing.com

Distributed by Macmillan, sales in Canada by The Canadian Manda Group.

24   23   22   21   20   1   2   3   4   5

ISBN-13: 978-1-64567-036-0

ISBN-10: 1-64567-036-8

Library of Congress Control Number: 2019951642

Cover and book design by Laura Benton for Page Street Publishing Co.

Photography by Charlotte Smythe

Printed and bound in China

TO MY GRANDMOTHER TOULIA.
Thank you for being so much more than just Grandma. Thank you for giving me a chance to dream. Thank you for never letting me down. But most of all, thank you for gifting me with the love of cooking. I couldn't imagine where I would be without your phenomenal soul. I love you so much.

TABLE OF CONTENTS

FOREWORD BY
DIANE SANFILIPPO

I first came to know Charlotte and her work as many of us likely did, through the ever-growing community of online recipe developers. But what made me tune in and connect with her on a deeper level is her story. Charlotte shares her passion and joy for not only the flavors in the dishes she develops, but also in her connection to her readers through sharing her life and her lifelong love of cooking.

Charlotte cooks from her heart and soul and shares those recipes so that her readers can feel her love and warmth straight through her food. She also goes the extra mile to spend time sharing about topics beyond food, which is such a breath of fresh air when we often need to be reminded of the three-dimensional, living, breathing people behind the recipes.

Gone are the days of collecting random lists of ingredients and processes without a heart and a voice attached to them—we all want food that is made with love, and created for us with our health goals in mind. As an avid recipe developer and cooking enthusiast myself, I know firsthand how challenging it can be to create amazing flavors for those following specific, often limiting dietary preferences.

In this book, Charlotte takes you on a culinary adventure, but in a way that simplifies it all. Amazing, bold flavors and a variety of dishes, but everything is, of course, in one pot, pan or dish.

Pull up a chair to Charlotte's table while she supports you in your Keto journey. You'll be glad you did.

DIANE SANFILIPPO,

New York Times bestselling author of *Practical Paleo*, *Keto Quick Start* and the *21-Day Sugar Detox* series

INTRODUCTION

HELLO and welcome to my Keto kitchen! The kitchen is very much my happy place, and cooking is my love language. I truly believe in the power of food. Food is comforting, healing and it brings us together. But I think many of us have been taught that choosing healthier options somehow means we have to sacrifice flavor, comfort and depth in our meals. Throughout my years of struggling with health and wellness, I had to learn that food is not an inhibitor: it is in fact my greatest weapon in finding a healthier me. The Keto diet is a perfect example of this fact. Instead of focusing on depriving myself, I've learned to embrace and value the right kind of foods that empower my body.

I am so happy to be a part of your journey to a better you. I know firsthand that deciding to make changes to your lifestyle takes a lot of courage, and it can be very challenging. Transitioning to the Keto diet is no different. You are choosing to put your health first, and we all need a little help sometimes. My hope is that these flavor-packed recipes will help you go about your day with a little more ease.

WHY ONE-POT DISHES?

When I first transitioned to the Keto diet, I found one-pot dishes to be my best friend. I lead a pretty busy lifestyle, and meal planning is necessary to keep me on track. With one-pot dishes, I can prep a few different dishes at a time to keep my meals fun and exciting for many days to come.

Simply put, one-pot dishes are essential for anyone who needs easy meals that don't take a lot of effort. And when you're transitioning to the Keto diet, you need uncomplicated meals that are versatile and tasty. I've had so much fun re-creating some of my favorite culturally rich dishes and making them Keto-friendly. I want to make sure you have dishes that are decadent and also make you feel good. So, this book is truly a labor of love packed with easy, fun recipes the whole family can enjoy together.

LET'S GET COOKING!

You will find that many one-pot dishes are very rich in culture and tradition. Being a very proud African, I can attest to that fact. But a lot of one-pot meals tend to be very decadent, and that doesn't necessarily align with the whole Keto diet thing. So, these recipes are a healthy balance of Keto-friendly goodness and the culturally rich flavors of many ethnic dishes.

Every recipe in this book was created with you in mind. For those days when you need dinner in no time, the Simple Minced Pork Noodles (page 40) is exactly what you need. And for those weekend nights when you have more time to spare, the Braised Mushroom Short Ribs (page 92) is the perfect place to start. These recipes emphasize simplicity and comfort, but add a flare of elegance with their depth of flavor.

So what are you waiting for? It's time to hop on the bus to flavor town with me right by your side! What are you going to make first? Turn the page and open up a world of phenomenal flavors created just for you.

xoxo,

9

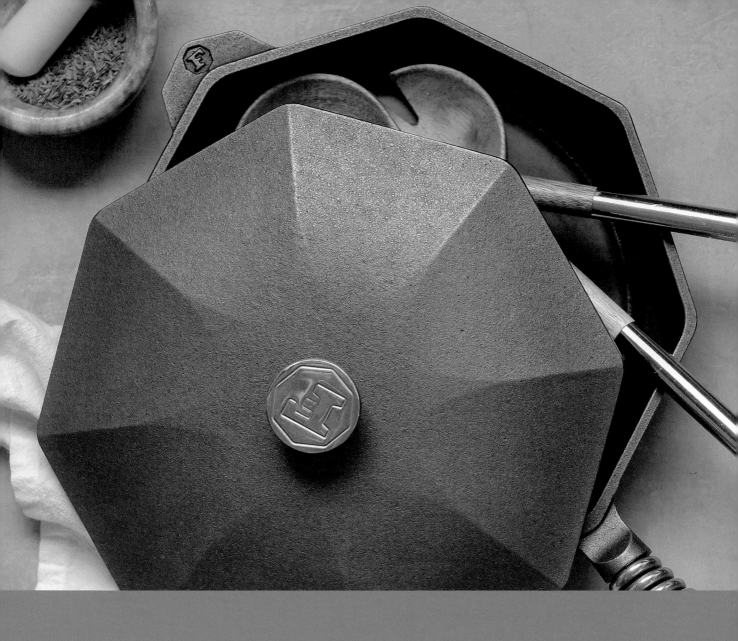

30-MINUTE
SKILLET MEALS

AFTER A LONG DAY, we all want and crave a meal that is ready in no time and does not skimp on flavor. This is exactly what these 30-minute skillet meals will provide for you and your family. They come together easily, there aren't a lot of crazy steps and they are packed with delicious flavors.

Recipes such as Easy Chicken Stir-Fry (page 15), Chili-Lime Steak Skillet (page 19) and Sizzling Seafood Paella (page 16) are fast and delicious, and they will also help you develop great kitchen skills. Although these recipes come together in a few easy steps, they also require prep work. So, it's a great time to get the whole family involved in the dinner prep.

Now, when it comes to your skillet, choose what you feel comfortable with. These meals will turn out just as delicious no matter the kind of skillet you use. But I do recommend getting your hands on a cast-iron skillet. There are a lot of great benefits to cooking with cast iron: the nonstick factor, the long lifespan and the fact that the skillet holds heat throughout the cooking process, which helps your food cook more evenly.

BEST-EVER SHRIMP
PAD THAI

What's better than a night in with takeout? How about a night in with a delicious, guilt-free takeout-inspired dish? Sounds good, right? Well, this insanely easy shrimp pad Thai is going to be your new favorite on takeout night! We are using Napa and red cabbage as our noodle substitute, along with a flavorful umami sauce and a nice crunch from the macadamia nuts. This is the low-carb guilty pleasure you have been waiting for.

2 tbsp (30 ml) fish sauce

2 tbsp (30 ml) coconut aminos

1 tbsp (15 ml) rice vinegar

1 tbsp (15 ml) harissa sauce (page 170)

¼ cup (60 ml) avocado oil, divided

½ lb (226 g) wild-caught shrimp, peeled and deveined with tails off

2 cloves garlic, grated

2 cups (140 g) shredded Napa cabbage

1 cup (70 g) shredded red or green cabbage

½ bell pepper, thinly sliced

¼ cup (33 g) roasted macadamia nuts, chopped and divided

Pinch of sea salt

Greens of 1 scallion, finely chopped, to garnish

To make the sauce, combine the fish sauce, coconut aminos, rice vinegar and harissa sauce in a bowl. Stir and set it aside.

Heat 2 tablespoons (30 ml) of avocado oil in a large skillet over medium-high heat. Sear the shrimp for 2 to 3 minutes on both sides. Remove the shrimp from the pan and set it aside.

Add the remaining avocado oil to the pan and stir in the garlic. Sauté the garlic until it is fragrant, about 1 minute. Then, add all of the cabbage and the bell pepper to the pan. Toss the vegetables in the garlic oil and sauté for about 3 minutes. Lower the heat to medium and return the shrimp to the pan along with the sauce and half of the macadamia nuts.

Toss all the ingredients together and continue to cook for 5 to 7 minutes, stirring frequently, until the cabbage is fork tender. Season with sea salt to taste. Garnish with the remaining macadamia nuts and the scallion.

PRO TIPS: If you want to use noodles in this dish instead of cabbage, I recommend using the zero-calorie shirataki noodles. You can find them at most grocery stores or online.

Not a fan of shrimp? You can use chicken, pork or steak instead.

EASY CHICKEN STIR-FRY

A stir-fry is an essential recipe to have in your back pocket. What I love about this recipe are the layers of umami flavor. The coconut aminos add some sweetness to the sauce, while the ginger adds a spicy kick. To bring it all together, the dried mushrooms add an extra layer of umami with their rich and complex notes.

SERVES
4

MACROS
Fat: 24.5 g
Carbs: 16.5 g
Net carbs: 13.4 g
Protein: 21.3 g
Fiber: 3.1 g

¼ cup (60 ml) coconut aminos

1 tsp apple cider vinegar

1 tbsp (15 ml) sesame oil

1 tsp grated ginger

¼ tsp crushed red pepper flakes

¼ tsp sea salt, plus more to taste

¼ tsp black pepper, plus more to taste

1 lb (454 g) boneless, skinless chicken thighs

1 oz (28 g) dried shiitake mushrooms

¼ cup (60 ml) avocado oil, divided

2 red bell peppers, julienned

1 bunch broccolini, trimmed

2 scallions, diced

2 cloves garlic, minced

Sesame seeds, to garnish

Cauliflower rice (page 154), to serve

To make the marinade, mix the coconut aminos, apple cider vinegar, sesame oil, ginger, crushed red pepper flakes, salt and pepper in a large bowl. Whisk to combine.

Pat the chicken thighs dry using a clean paper towel and cut them into 1-inch (2.5-cm) chunks. Add the chicken thighs to the bowl with the marinade and toss the chicken to make sure it's well coated with the marinade. Set the chicken aside to marinate for 7 to 10 minutes.

Put the mushrooms in a bowl and cover them with warm water. Let them sit for 7 to 10 minutes to rehydrate, then cut the larger pieces into two to three pieces.

Heat a large wok or skillet over high heat. Once the pan starts to smoke, lower the heat to medium, add 1 tablespoon (15 ml) of avocado oil and cook the bell peppers for 2 to 3 minutes. Season with salt and pepper. Remove the peppers from the pan and set them aside. Add another tablespoon (15 ml) of avocado oil to the pan and cook the broccolini for 2 to 3 minutes. Season with a pinch of salt and pepper. Remove it from the pan and set it aside. Add another tablespoon (15 ml) of avocado oil and cook the mushrooms for 2 minutes and set them aside.

Add the last tablespoon (15 ml) of avocado oil to the hot pan and dump the chicken and marinade into the pan. Increase the heat to high and cook the chicken for 3 to 5 minutes, until it's nicely brown and cooked through. Add the scallions and garlic to the pan and continue to cook for 1 minute. Return the peppers, broccolini and mushrooms to the pan. Continue to cook until the vegetables have a nice coating of sauce, about 3 minutes. Garnish with sesame seeds and serve over cauliflower rice.

PRO TIP: If you're meal planning, make the marinade, pour it into a ziplock bag and add the chicken. Massage the bag to coat the chicken with the marinade. Store the chicken in the fridge for the next day or freeze it for a later date. If frozen, thaw the chicken in the fridge overnight.

SERVES
4

MACROS
Fat: 16.7 g
Carbs: 11.5 g
Net carbs:
8.1 g
Protein:
21.2 g
Fiber: 3.4 g

SIZZLING SEAFOOD PAELLA

If you've never heard of paella, it is a Spanish dish that is very rich in history and culture. It's similar to jambalaya in how it's prepared, but the flavors are more Spanish than Cajun. Paella is usually cooked with saffron to give it a rich yellow color, but we will use turmeric instead because it's milder and pairs well with the cauliflower rice. Paella may seem a little intimidating because of its beauty and vibrant colors, but making it is deliciously simple and easy. In just a few steps, this Keto-friendly version is nothing short of incredible.

2 tbsp (30 ml) avocado oil, divided

4 oz (113 g) no-sugar-added Cajun sausage, sliced

1 shallot, finely chopped

2 cloves garlic, finely minced

1 (14.5-oz [411-g]) can fire-roasted diced tomatoes

2 (10-oz [283-g]) bags frozen cauliflower rice

1 tsp ground turmeric

1 tsp Italian seasoning

½ tsp sea salt

1 tsp fish sauce

½ lb (226 g) raw shrimp, peeled and deveined with tails on

½ lb (226 g) fresh clams

1 tbsp (15 ml) melted unsalted butter

¼ tsp crushed red pepper flakes

Chopped scallions, lemon juice and lemon wedges, to serve

Heat 1 tablespoon (15 ml) of avocado oil in a large paella pan or a deep 12-inch (30-cm) skillet over medium-high heat. Add the sausage and brown it for 2 to 3 minutes. Remove the sausage from the pan and set it aside.

Add the other tablespoon (15 ml) of avocado oil to the same pan and sauté the shallot and garlic until the garlic is fragrant, about 1 minute. Pour the tomatoes into the pan and stir to lift all the brown bits from the bottom of the pan.

Add the cauliflower rice, turmeric, Italian seasoning, salt and fish sauce to the pan and toss until all the ingredients are well combined. Return the sausage to the pan and toss it with the rest of the ingredients. Simmer the paella for 5 to 7 minutes, until most of the liquid from the cauliflower rice has evaporated. Add the shrimp and clams, tucking them into the cauliflower rice mixture. Drizzle the butter all over the shrimp and clams and sprinkle the crushed red pepper flakes on top. Cover the paella pan with aluminum foil and simmer until the shrimp is cooked through and the clams open, about 8 to 10 minutes.

Sprinkle the scallions over the top, squeeze some lemon juice over the seafood and serve immediately with lemon wedges.

CHILI-LIME STEAK SKILLET

SERVES
4

MACROS

Fat: 22.8 g

Carbs: 8.1 g

Net carbs:
6.1 g

Protein:
25.3 g

Fiber: 2 g

A juicy sizzling steak dinner without the steakhouse prices—I think yes! Impress your loved ones with this ready-in-no-time meal that will knock their socks off. The key to this dish is the tangy, slightly sweet marinade that will take any cut of steak to a whole new level of flavor town. For a heartier meal, try adding more vegetables such as mushrooms or broccoli.

2 tbsp (30 ml) avocado oil

Juice of 1 small lime

3 cloves garlic, finely minced

1 tbsp (15 ml) coconut aminos

1 tsp sea salt

2 tbsp (2 g) finely chopped fresh cilantro leaves

½ tsp crushed red pepper flakes

1 lb (454 g) steak (skirt, flank, rib eye)

2 tbsp (26 g) organic grass-fed ghee, divided

2 red bell peppers, sliced

1 onion, sliced

Avocado slices and lime wedges, to serve

To make the marinade, whisk the avocado oil, lime juice, garlic, coconut aminos, salt, cilantro and crushed red pepper flakes in a small bowl. Pour half the marinade in a shallow dish and add the steak. Toss the steak with the marinade and let it sit for 10 minutes. If time allows, you can marinate the steak overnight.

Heat 1 tablespoon (13 g) of ghee in a cast-iron pan over medium-high heat until the ghee starts to smoke. Add the steak and sear it for 3 to 5 minutes on both sides for medium rare or 5 to 7 minutes for medium. Remove the steak from the pan and set it aside.

To the same pan, add the other tablespoon (13 g) of ghee and sauté the peppers and onion for about 5 to 7 minutes, until they are fork tender. Remove the vegetables from the heat and toss with half of the leftover marinade.

Slice the steak against the grain and finish it off with the rest of the untouched marinade. Serve the steak and vegetables with avocado slices and lime wedges.

MACROS
Fat: 27.6 g

Carbs: 2.9 g

Net carbs:
2.3 g

Protein:
22.5 g

Fiber: 0.6 g

GRILLED SWORDFISH IN
CITRUS-HERB SAUCE

If you just aren't sure how you feel about seafood, then this is the fish I want you to cook up immediately! Swordfish is the perfect fish for anyone who hasn't had a lot of experience with seafood. It's very mild so it will absorb any flavors you add to it. The meaty and mild swordfish served with this citrus-infused herb sauce will take your taste buds to a whole new world. You can also try cod or halibut in the dish. Serve it with grilled peppers, a salad or broccolini (page 157).

2 tbsp (30 ml) olive oil

1 tbsp (15 ml) lime juice

1 tbsp (15 ml) lemon juice

2 tbsp (30 ml) coconut aminos

2 tbsp (2 g) chopped fresh cilantro leaves

1 tbsp (6 g) chopped fresh mint leaves

2 cloves garlic, finely minced

¼ tsp crushed red pepper flakes

2 (6-oz [170-g]) swordfish steaks

Sea salt and black pepper

2 tbsp (30 ml) melted organic grass-fed ghee, divided

1 large red bell pepper, deseeded and quartered

Lemon slices, to serve

To make the citrus sauce, combine the olive oil, lime juice, lemon juice, coconut aminos, cilantro, mint, garlic and crushed red pepper flakes in a bowl. Mix well. Set the sauce aside.

Prepare a grill or a grill pan by heating it over medium-high heat. Pat the swordfish steaks dry and season them with salt and pepper on both sides.

When the grill/grill pan is hot, brush it with 1 tablespoon (13 ml) of ghee. Add the swordfish steaks to the hot grill/grill pan. Cook the fish for 3 to 4 minutes per side, depending on how thick your steak is. Remove the fish from the pan and set it aside to rest. Brush the other tablespoon (13 ml) of ghee onto the grill/grill pan. Grill the bell pepper for 5 to 8 minutes, or until the pepper pieces begin to blister and soften.

Pour the citrus sauce over the fish and pepper pieces, and serve with lemon slices.

HEARTY CHICKEN
CACCIATORE

What I absolutely love about Italian dishes is the versatility and simplicity. You just need a few key ingredients such as tomatoes, good olive oil, herbs, braising liquid and your protein of choice—plus a few staples you already have in your kitchen, such as onions and garlic. And that's it! Simple ingredients that turn into a warm, comforting and hearty dish. Serve with zucchini noodles (page 161) or fluffy cauliflower rice (page 154).

SERVES
4

MACROS
Fat: 17.8 g
Carbs: 11.1 g
Net carbs: 7.6 g
Protein: 21.2 g
Fiber: 3.5 g

3 tbsp (45 ml) olive oil, divided

1 lb (454 g) boneless, skinless chicken thighs

1 tsp sea salt, plus more to taste

1 tsp black pepper, plus more to taste

1 onion, diced

4 cloves garlic, finely minced

1 tbsp (16 g) tomato paste

¼ cup (60 ml) Chicken Bone Broth (page 166) or store-bought

1 (14.5-oz [411-g]) can fire-roasted diced tomatoes

1 tsp capers

Chopped basil leaves, to garnish

Heat 2 tablespoons (30 ml) of olive oil in a large, deep skillet or Dutch oven over medium-high heat.

Pat the chicken thighs dry using a clean paper towel. Season the chicken on both sides with the salt and black pepper. Add the chicken to the hot pan and sear for 3 to 5 minutes on both sides. Remove the chicken from the pan and set it aside.

Add the remaining tablespoon (15 ml) of olive oil to same pan along with the onion and garlic. Sauté the onion and garlic, stirring frequently, for 5 to 7 minutes until the onion is tender. Stir in the tomato paste and continue to cook for about 2 minutes. Pour in the broth and stir to lift up all the yummy bits and pieces from the bottom of the pan. Add the tomatoes to the pan.

Give the sauce a quick stir and nestle the chicken pieces into the sauce. Sprinkle the capers over the chicken, cover the pan and continue to simmer for 7 to 10 minutes. Remove the cover and simmer for 5 minutes to thicken the sauce.

Adjust salt and pepper, if desired, and garnish with fresh basil leaves.

MACROS:
Fat: 17.5 g
Carbs: 16.1 g
Net carbs:
13.5 g
Protein:
2.6 g
Fiber: 2.6 g

FALL HARVEST STIR-FRY

During the cold months, I especially love whipping up stir-fries with warm savory vegetables and flavors. This dish is the perfect combination of fall flavors with earthy mushrooms and broccolini paired with buttery, slightly sweet butternut squash. If you are a meat lover, trust me, you will not miss the meat in this dish. If you do, serve this with Braised Mushroom Short Ribs (page 92).

¼ cup (60 ml) avocado oil, divided

1 cup (140 g) peeled and diced butternut squash (½-inch [1-cm] cubes)

1 bell pepper, sliced

Sea salt and black pepper

4 tbsp (60 ml) Chicken Bone Broth (page 166) or store-bought, divided

1 bunch broccolini

4 oz (113 g) shiitake mushrooms

2 cloves garlic, minced

2 tbsp (30 ml) coconut aminos

1 tsp fish sauce

1 tbsp (15 ml) sesame oil

Crushed red pepper flakes, to garnish

Thai basil, to garnish

Heat a large nonstick skillet over medium-high heat and pour in 2 tablespoons (30 ml) of avocado oil. Add the butternut squash and bell pepper and sauté for about 5 minutes, stirring continuously. Season with a couple pinches of salt and black pepper, add 2 tablespoons (30 ml) of broth and cover the pan. Lower the heat to medium. Cook the squash and pepper for 10 to 12 minutes, stirring continuously, until the squash is fork tender and almost completely cooked through. Remove the squash and bell pepper from the pan and set them aside.

Lower the heat to medium-low, add 1 tablespoon (15 ml) of avocado oil to the skillet and add the broccolini. Toss the broccolini and sauté for 1 to 2 minutes, then season with salt and pepper. Add the remaining 2 tablespoons (30 ml) of broth to the pan, cover the pan and let the broccolini cook for 3 to 5 minutes. Remove the broccolini from the pan and set it aside.

Increase the heat to medium and add the remaining tablespoon (15 ml) of avocado oil along with the mushrooms and garlic to the pan. Season with salt and pepper and sauté for 3 to 5 minutes.

Return the squash, bell pepper and broccolini to the pan. Add the coconut aminos, fish sauce and sesame oil to the pan. Toss all the ingredients together and continue to sauté for 2 to 3 minutes to marry all the flavors. Garnish with the pepper flakes and Thai basil. Serve immediately.

WONTON BALLS AND
MARINATED SCALLIONS

SERVES
6

MACROS
Fat: 25 g
Carbs: 8.8 g
Net carbs: 8.7 g
Protein: 19.7 g
Fiber: 0.1 g

This dish has become a huge hit in my house, and I knew I had to share it with you. What I love about these flavor bomb balls is that you can use them as part of a meal, but they are also wonderful for entertaining. They are incredibly tasty and make the perfect finger food for any party. Just pop them in an air fryer, and in no time, you are ready to get the party started with wonton balls. If you don't eat pork, you can try substituting chicken or turkey.

½ oz (14 g) dried shiitake mushrooms

1 lb (454 g) ground pork

½ cup (35 g) finely chopped Napa cabbage leaves

2 tbsp (2 g) finely chopped fresh cilantro leaves

4 cloves garlic, finely minced, divided

½ tsp sea salt

½ tsp black pepper

3 tbsp (45 ml) avocado oil, divided

1 tbsp (15 ml) sesame oil

1 tsp fish sauce

1 tsp rice vinegar

2 tbsp (30 ml) coconut aminos

3 scallions, finely chopped

½ tsp crushed red pepper flakes

Add the dried mushrooms to a bowl of warm water. Set them aside to rehydrate for about 15 to 30 minutes. Remove the mushrooms from the water, squeeze out any excess liquid and chop them very finely.

Transfer the mushrooms to a mixing bowl along with the ground pork, cabbage, cilantro, half of the garlic, sea salt and black pepper. Use a fork to gently mix the meat mixture until it's well combined; do not overmix. Use a small cookie scoop to scoop out equal amounts of the meat mixture, roll them into balls using your hands and transfer them to a tray lined with parchment paper. You should be able to make 12 to 15 balls from the meat mixture.

To make the marinated scallions, add the remaining garlic to a bowl along with 1 tablespoon (15 ml) of avocado oil, the sesame oil, fish sauce, rice vinegar, coconut aminos, scallions and crushed red pepper flakes. Stir the mixture and set it aside.

Spray an air fryer basket with avocado oil spray and add the meatballs to the basket, making sure they do not touch. Do this in batches if your air fryer basket is not large enough to fit all the meatballs at once. Cook in the air fryer at 375°F (190°C) for 12 to 15 minutes, depending on your air fryer.

Remove the meatballs from the air fryer. Scatter the marinated scallions over the wonton balls and serve hot.

PRO TIP: To cook this dish in the oven, transfer the rolled meatballs to a prepared sheet pan sprayed with avocado oil spray. Cook the meatballs in a preheated oven at 400°F (200°C, or gas mark 6) for 15 to 20 minutes, turning once. Then serve them with the marinated scallions.

SERVES

4

MACROS

Fat: 21 g

Carbs: 9.5 g

Net carbs:
6.1 g

Protein: 16.1 g

Fiber: 3.4 g

CAJUN CHICKEN AND
GREEN BEANS

Chicken thighs are my absolute favorite cut of the chicken. So, I thoroughly enjoy showing off their juicy tenderness every chance I get. These chicken thighs are crisped up and then finished with warm Cajun spices. The green beans are the perfect addition to this dish, because they cut through the richness of the thigh and give you a fresh bite.

1 lb (454 g) bone-in, skin-on chicken thighs

Sea salt and black pepper

1 tbsp (13 g) organic grass-fed ghee

1 tbsp (15 ml) lemon juice

2 tbsp (30 ml) melted unsalted butter

1 tsp paprika

¼ tsp cayenne pepper

¼ tsp onion powder

½ tsp garlic powder

1 lb (454 g) fresh or frozen green beans

2 lemon slices

Preheat the oven to 425°F (220°C, or gas mark 7).

Trim the chicken thighs of any excess skin and fat. Pat them dry using paper towels and season them with a few generous pinches of salt and pepper on both sides.

Heat the ghee in a large cast-iron or oven-safe skillet over high heat. Once the pan starts to smoke, lower the heat to medium-high and add the chicken thighs to the pan skin side down. Sear the chicken for 7 minutes, or until the skin is brown and crispy. With the chicken still skin side down, transfer the skillet to the preheated oven and continue to cook the chicken for 7 minutes.

While the chicken is in the oven, combine the lemon juice, butter, paprika, cayenne pepper, onion powder and garlic powder in a small bowl.

Remove the skillet from the oven, flip the chicken thighs and push them to one side of the skillet. Put the green beans on a large sheet of aluminum foil and nestle it next to the chicken in the pan. Drizzle the butter mixture all over the chicken and green beans. Nestle the lemon slices between the chicken thighs. Season the green beans with salt and pepper, then fold the long ends of the foil over the beans, and pinch the shorter ends to close the packet. Return the skillet to the oven. Continue to cook for 15 minutes, or until the chicken is cooked through and the green beans are fork tender.

HARISSA PORK CHOPS
AND SQUASH

SERVES
4

MACROS
Fat: 10.9 g
Carbs: 6.1 g
Net carbs:
4.7 g
Protein:
23.7 g
Fiber: 1.4 g

When I talk about simple and easy meals, this dish is a perfect example of just that. It's quick and easy and only requires a few simple ingredients. One of those is harissa sauce. Harissa is an ingredient you will see repeated throughout this book, because it adds so much flavor and spice to anything you are cooking. Boneless pork chops tend to be very lean and can sometimes be a little harder to season. Adding a rich flavor-booster such as harissa simply brings the pork chop to life.

1 zucchini

1 yellow squash

4 boneless pork chops

Sea salt and black pepper

2 tbsp (26 g) organic grass-fed ghee

2 cloves garlic, finely minced

2 tbsp (30 ml) harissa sauce (page 170)

2 tbsp (30 ml) coconut aminos

Preheat the oven to broil.

Cut the zucchini in half lengthwise and then cut it into ¼-inch (6-mm) slices. Repeat with the yellow squash. Set them aside.

Season the pork chops with a couple pinches of salt and pepper on both sides.

Heat the ghee in a large oven-safe skillet over medium-high heat. Sear the pork chops for 2 to 3 minutes on both sides. Remove the chops from the pan and set them aside. Add the zucchini, yellow squash and garlic to the same pan and sauté the vegetables for 3 to 5 minutes. Return the pork chops to the pan and nestle them between the zucchini slices.

Mix the harissa and coconut aminos together in a small bowl. Pour the mixture over the pork chops and transfer the skillet to the preheated oven. Broil for 5 minutes.

Remove the skillet from the oven and let the chops rest for a few minutes before serving.

SERVES
4

MACROS

Fat: 18.4 g

Carbs: 11.4 g

Net carbs:
11.3 g

Protein:
29.6 g

Fiber: 0.1 g

VIETNAMESE PORK
AND CABBAGE

Pork and cabbage may sound a little boring, right? Well not this pork and cabbage. The thinly sliced pork is rubbed with an array of rich, warm spices and then pan-seared to perfection. The lightly sautéed cabbage, paired with the rich flavor of the pork, adds a nice balance to the dish. Finish with fresh scallions and Thai basil if you can find it.

---

1 small head Napa cabbage

1 tbsp (15 ml) sesame oil

1 shallot, diced

4 cloves garlic, finely minced

1 tbsp (6 g) grated ginger

½ tsp crushed red pepper flakes

1 lb (454 g) thinly sliced pork shoulder

1 tbsp (15 ml) fish sauce

2 tbsp (30 ml) coconut aminos

Sea salt and black pepper

Scallions and Thai basil, to serve

Cut 2 inches (5 cm) off the bottom of the cabbage. Run the cabbage leaves under cold water to remove any dirt and slice it into shreds. Set it aside.

Heat the sesame oil in a large skillet over medium-high heat. Add the shallot, garlic, ginger and crushed red pepper flakes. Sauté the aromatics for about 2 minutes, until the garlic is fragrant.

Add the pork to the pan. Cook for 5 to 7 minutes, until the pork is cooked through and starts to develop some color. Add the fish sauce and coconut aminos and continue to cook, stirring frequently, for 5 minutes. Remove the pork from the pan and set it aside.

Lower the heat and add the cabbage to the same pan. Toss the cabbage and sauté for 3 to 5 minutes, until the cabbage begins to wilt. Season with salt and pepper to taste. Return the pork to the pan and toss to combine with the cabbage. Garnish with scallions and Thai basil.

CRISPY SALMON AND 5-INGREDIENT TARTAR SAUCE

Forget the wait list at your favorite restaurant. You can enjoy crispy, juicy salmon in minutes in the comfort of your own home. This dish is pretty much foolproof. All you need to do is allow the fish enough time to develop a nice crust. You can use either skin-on or skinless salmon according to your preferences. The creamy and tangy tartar sauce paired with the rich, buttery flavor of the salmon is complete bliss.

SERVES
4

MACROS
Fat: 37 g
Carbs: 4.3 g
Net carbs: 2.3 g
Protein: 26.7 g
Fiber: 2 g

½ cup (120 ml) avocado mayonnaise

1 tsp yellow mustard

1 tbsp (15 ml) lemon juice

1 tbsp (15 g) diced organic no-sugar-added dill pickles

1 tsp capers, minced

Sea salt and black pepper

3 tbsp (39 g) organic grass-fed ghee, divided

4 salmon fillets

1 bunch asparagus, trimmed

2 tbsp (30 ml) Chicken Bone Broth (page 166) or store-bought

Lemon wedges, to serve

To make the tartar sauce, add the avocado mayo, yellow mustard, lemon juice, pickles and capers to a small bowl. Whisk all the ingredients together to combine. Season with a pinch of salt and pepper to taste. Transfer the tartar sauce to the fridge until you're ready to serve.

Heat a 12-inch (30-cm) cast-iron skillet over high heat until the pan begins to smoke. Lower the heat to medium-high and melt 2 tablespoons (26 g) of ghee in the pan.

Pat the salmon dry with clean paper towels and season with a couple pinches of salt and pepper. Transfer the fish to the hot pan flesh side down. Sear the fish for 5 minutes. Flip the fish. If you are having a hard time flipping the fish, let it sear for 2 minutes more then try again. Sear for 2 minutes on the other side. Remove the fish from the pan and set it aside.

Add the remaining tablespoon (13 g) of ghee to the skillet and sauté the asparagus for about 2 to 3 minutes. Add the bone broth and continue to cook the asparagus for 2 to 3 minutes. Season with a couple pinches of salt and pepper to taste. Remove the asparagus from the heat and return the salmon to the pan. Serve with the tartar sauce and lemon wedges on the side.

PRO TIP: If you have a hard time finding pickles that do not contain any sugar, here are two brands I recommend: The Grillo's Pickles brand, sold at Target, and the Thrive Market brand dill pickles.

MACROS
Fat: 60.1 g

Carbs: 0.9 g

Net carbs:
0.8 g

Protein:
16.7 g

Fiber: 0.1 g

SPICY STIR-FRY
KIMCHI AND PORK

This dish is inspired by one I had at one of my favorite Asian spots in Minnesota. The first time I had it, the bursting flavor hit me like a ton of bricks. The juicy and tender pork belly paired with the sour, spicy and umami flavor of the kimchi makes this dish incredibly special. Serve over cauliflower rice (page 154) with fresh cucumbers for a complete meal.

2 cups (480 ml) Chicken Bone Broth (page 166) or store-bought

1 lb (454 g) pork belly, cut in ½-inch (1-cm) slices

½ tsp Chinese five-spice

¼ tsp sea salt

1½ cups (360 g) no-sugar-added kimchi

1 tbsp (15 ml) coconut aminos

2 scallions, chopped with whites and greens separated

Heat the broth in a deep skillet over medium-high heat and bring it to a simmer. Add the pork belly, cover the pan and simmer for 5 to 7 minutes. Remove the pork from the pan and transfer it to a cutting board. Save ¼ cup (60 ml) of the broth and discard the rest.

Cut the pork belly slices into thirds. Sprinkle the Chinese five-spice and salt over the pork belly and toss to coat. Return the skillet to the heat and add the pork belly pieces. Sear the pork belly for 5 to 7 minutes on both sides. Remove the pork belly from the heat and transfer it to a plate lined with paper towels. Discard the pork belly fat and return the skillet to the heat.

Place the kimchi in the skillet, sauté for 3 to 5 minutes and stir in the coconut aminos. Continue to sauté for 1 to 2 minutes, then deglaze the pan with the ¼ cup (60 ml) of reserved broth. Continue to simmer for 2 to 3 minutes.

Return the pork belly to the skillet along with the whites of the scallions and toss with the kimchi mixture. Garnish with the greens of the scallions and serve.

5-INGREDIENT
SHRIMP ALFREDO

SERVES

2

MACROS

Fat: 40.4 g

Carbs: 8.8 g

Net carbs: 6.7 g

Protein: 20.9 g

Fiber: 2.1 g

After you've had a long day, you just need simplicity when it comes to dinner. That's exactly where five-ingredient meals come in. This creamy and decadent shrimp alfredo is perfect for date night or nights when you just need some comfort food. I did not count the butter, salt, pepper and herb garnish in the ingredient number because these are kitchen staples.

2 zucchinis, spiralized

½ tsp sea salt, plus more to taste

2 tbsp (28 g) butter

½ lb (226 g) wild-caught shrimp, peeled and deveined with tails on

Black pepper

2 cloves garlic, finely minced

½ cup (120 ml) heavy cream

¼ cup (25 g) grated Parmesan cheese

Fresh parsley, to garnish

Put the spiralized zucchini noodles in a bowl lined with cheesecloth. Sprinkle ½ teaspoon of salt all over the noodles and let them sit for about 15 minutes. After 15 minutes, wrap the cheesecloth around the noodles and squeeze to get the excess liquid out of the zucchini. Set the noodles aside.

Heat the butter in a large skillet over medium-high heat. Season the shrimp with a couple pinches of salt and pepper. Transfer the shrimp to the heated skillet and sear for 2 to 3 minutes on both sides. Remove the shrimp from the pan and set it aside

Add the garlic to the pan and sauté for 1 to 2 minutes. Slowly add the heavy cream to the pan and simmer for 3 to 5 minutes, stirring occasionally. Add the zucchini noodles along with the Parmesan cheese to the pan. Toss to combine. Return the shrimp and all of its juices to the pan and toss to combine with the pasta.

At this point, season with salt and pepper to taste and garnish with fresh parsley.

PRO TIP: For a dairy-free option, use full-fat coconut milk instead of heavy cream. You can also omit the Parmesan cheese and use nutritional yeast for a cheesy, nutty flavor.

SIMPLE MINCED PORK
NOODLES

SERVES
4

MACROS
Fat: 24.2 g
Carbs: 11 g
Net carbs:
8.4 g
Protein:
20.1 g
Fiber: 2.6 g

There is no better way to satisfy all your takeout cravings than with a warm bowl of noodles. This quick and easy dish packs a lot of flavor without having a long list of ingredients. Most of the ingredients are pantry staples so you can be on your way to a crowd-pleasing dinner in no time.

---

3 large zucchinis, spiralized

Sea salt

1 lb (454 g) ground pork

1 tbsp (15 ml) sesame oil

1 shallot, finely chopped

2 cloves garlic, minced

1 tsp ginger

¼ cup (60 ml) coconut aminos

2 tbsp (30 ml) no-sugar-added BBQ sauce

1 tsp golden monk fruit sweetener

1 tsp crushed red pepper flakes

Black pepper

Chopped scallions and sesame seeds, to garnish

Transfer the spiralized zucchini noodles to a large bowl lined with cheesecloth. Sprinkle a few pinches of salt over the noodles and set aside.

Heat a deep skillet over medium-high heat and add the ground pork. Cook the pork until it is no longer pink and starts to develop a nice brown crust, about 7 minutes. Add the sesame oil, shallot, garlic and ginger to the pan. Continue to cook the pork and the aromatics for another 5 minutes until the shallot is tender.

To make the sauce, combine the coconut aminos, BBQ sauce, sweetener and crushed red pepper flakes to a small bowl and mix well. Pour half of the sauce over the pork and sauté for about 2 minutes, stirring continuously.

Wrap the cheesecloth around the zucchini noodles and squeeze to get all of the excess liquid out of the noodles. Increase the heat to high, and add the noodles to the pan. Toss the noodles with the pork mixture for about 2 minutes. Lower the heat to medium-high, then pour the rest of the sauce over the noodles and pork and continue to sauté, stirring continuously, for 2 to 3 minutes.

Taste and season the mixture with salt and pepper if necessary. Garnish with scallions and sesame seeds, and serve immediately.

PRO TIP: If you are not a fan of zucchini noodles, try using shirataki noodles. You can also use cooked spaghetti squash for a heartier meal.

CREAMY SALMON PICCATA

SERVES
4

MACROS
Fat: 23.3 g
Carbs: 3.1 g
Net carbs:
3 g
Protein:
25.7 g
Fiber: 0.1 g

One of my favorite meals growing up was chicken piccata. I love the creamy, tangy sauce. So, I decided to put a fun twist on this masterpiece of a dish by using rich pieces of salmon instead of chicken. Let me tell you, it has officially changed my life. The buttery flavor of the salmon cuts right through the lemon sauce, making every sensational bite a little bit better than the last.

4 salmon fillets, skin-on

Sea salt and black pepper

1 tbsp (13 g) organic grass-fed ghee

1 tbsp (15 ml) olive oil

2 cloves garlic, finely minced

⅓ cup (80 ml) Chicken Bone Broth (page 166) or store-bought

2 tbsp (30 ml) lemon juice

½ cup (120 ml) heavy cream

2 tbsp (17 g) capers, drained and rinsed

Fresh basil, to garnish

Pat the salmon fillets dry and season with salt and pepper.

Heat the ghee and olive oil in a large skillet over medium-high heat and add the salmon skin side down. Sear the salmon for 3 minutes on both sides. Remove the fish from the pan and set it aside.

Lower the heat to medium and add the garlic. Sauté until the garlic is fragrant, about 1 minute. Stir in the broth and lemon juice, and simmer for 1 minute. Slowly stir in the cream and simmer for 2 minutes.

Return the salmon to the sauce and add the capers. Continue to simmer for 2 to 3 minutes, or until the sauce thickens. Garnish with fresh basil.

PRO TIP: For a dairy-free option, simply omit the ghee and use another tablespoon (15 ml) of olive oil and use full-fat coconut milk instead of heavy cream.

CHICKEN TERIYAKI
FRIED RICE

Fried rice is always on everyone's list when it comes to Chinese takeout. It's hearty with layers of flavor, and everyone loves it. That is exactly the case with this teriyaki fried rice. Although we are using cauliflower rice, this dish is still very hearty and it does not disappoint when it comes to flavor. You can easily double the recipe to feed more people.

¼ cup (60 ml) coconut aminos

1 tsp grated ginger

1 tsp garlic powder

1 tbsp (15 ml) sesame oil

1 tsp golden monk fruit sweetener

½ tsp crushed red pepper flakes

3 tbsp (45 ml) avocado oil, divided

½ lb (226 g) boneless skinless chicken thighs, cut into strips

Sea salt and black pepper

1 bell pepper, cut into ½-inch (1-cm) cubes

1 onion, cut into ½-inch (1-cm) cubes

5 oz (142 g) sliced portobello mushrooms

1 (12-oz [340-g]) bag frozen cauliflower rice

1 scallion, finely chopped

To make the sauce, mix the coconut aminos, ginger, garlic powder, sesame oil, sweetener and crushed red pepper flakes in a small bowl. Stir to combine and set it aside.

Heat a nonstick skillet over medium-high heat and add 2 tablespoons (30 ml) of avocado oil. Season the chicken thighs with salt and pepper and add them to the hot skillet. Sear the chicken for about 2 to 3 minutes per side.

Remove the chicken from the pan and set it aside. Add the bell pepper, onion and mushrooms to the pan. Drizzle the remaining tablespoon (15 ml) of avocado oil over the vegetables and sauté, stirring frequently for 5 to 7 minutes. Season with salt and pepper.

Now return the chicken to the pan and pour the sauce into the pan. Continue to sauté, stirring frequently, for 2 minutes, until the sauce begins to thicken. Then stir in the frozen cauliflower rice and increase the heat to high. Toss the cauliflower with the rest of the ingredients. Sauté for 5 to 7 minutes, or until the cauliflower is tender and all the liquid has evaporated.

Taste and season the cauliflower mixture with more salt and pepper if necessary. Add the scallion to the fried rice and give it a gentle toss. Serve immediately.

ITALIAN SAUSAGE AND PEPPERS

SERVES
4

MACROS
Fat: 13 g
Carbs: 11.7 g
Net carbs:
8.5 g
Fiber: 3.2 g
Protein:
19.2 g

This classic Italian-American street food is bursting with deep, rich flavors, and you won't believe how quickly and easily it comes together. To make the dish a little heartier, I decided to add portobello mushrooms. They add extra meaty flavor and texture to the dish.

2 tbsp (30 ml) avocado oil

10 oz (283 g) sweet Italian sausage links, cut into thirds

1 onion, sliced

1 red bell pepper, sliced

1 green bell pepper, sliced

5 oz (142 g) portobello mushrooms, sliced

Sea salt and black pepper

1 tsp Italian seasoning

½ tsp garlic powder

1 tsp smoked paprika

¼ tsp crushed red pepper flakes

1 tbsp (16 g) tomato paste

½ cup (120 ml) Chicken Bone Broth (page 166) or store-bought

Basil leaves, to garnish

Cauliflower rice (page 154), to serve

Heat a large skillet over medium-high heat. Add the avocado oil to the pan and sear the sausage pieces for about 3 minutes on each side. Remove the sausage from the pan and set it aside.

Add the onion, bell peppers and mushrooms to the pan. Sauté the vegetables for about 5 minutes and season with a few pinches of salt and pepper. Continue to cook the vegetables for another 5 to 7 minutes until the peppers have softened. Then add the Italian seasoning, garlic powder, paprika, crushed red pepper flakes and tomato paste to the pan. Stir all the ingredients together and continue to cook for 1 minute.

Pour the broth into the pan and stir to lift up any brown bits from the bottom of the pan. Return the sausage to the pan, stir and turn the heat to medium-low. Simmer the mixture for about 3 minutes just to heat the sausage through. Garnish with fresh basil leaves and serve with cauliflower rice.

NO MESS SHEET-PAN DINNERS

WHEN I WAS FIRST INTRODUCED to the world of sheet-pan dinners, I enjoyed it mostly because it meant I wouldn't have much cleaning up to do after a meal. But now, as I continue to fall in love with sheet-pan dinners, I have come to love how creative, easy and fun they are!

One thing I really want to accomplish with these recipes is to give you new ideas. Bruschetta Chicken and Squash (page 54), Sheet-Pan Jambalaya (page 70), Salmon Niçoise Salad with Mustard Dressing (page 58) and Sheet-Pan Kung Pao Chicken (page 61) are just a few recipes that are not your "traditional" sheet-pan dinners. I want to give you fresh ideas that you can have fun re-creating with your whole family.

But, for those busy weeknights, Mini Meatloaf Dinner (page 57), 5-Ingredient Chicken and Asparagus (page 69) and Glazed Teriyaki Salmon (page 77) are just a few examples of quick and easy sheet-pan dinners you can have on the table in little to no time.

You will also notice I use aluminum foil or parchment paper in a lot of these recipes for even easier clean up. In many cases, because we are cooking the protein at high oven temperatures, wrapping your vegetables in foil or parchment paper is a great way to cook the vegetables without burning them.

SERVES

6

MACROS

Fat: 19.8 g

Carbs: 1.4 g

Net carbs:
1.1 g

Protein:
24.8 g

Fiber: 0.3 g

BLACKENED SALMON
WITH CHIMICHURRI

My relationship with salmon is a very loving one. Although it is rich in good fats, salmon is very subtle and refreshing. I love keeping things simple when it comes to salmon, but I also love pairing it with warm flavors. Here we use a Cajun rub with a fresh herb sauce to cut through all those rich flavors.

1½ lb (680 g) salmon fillet

2 tbsp (30 ml) melted unsalted butter

½ tsp sea salt, plus more to taste

1 tsp smoked paprika

½ tsp onion powder

½ tsp garlic powder

½ tsp cayenne pepper

1 tbsp (15 ml) lemon juice

¼ cup (60 ml) olive oil

2 tbsp (2 g) finely chopped fresh cilantro leaves

2 tbsp (8 g) finely chopped fresh parsley leaves

1 tbsp (6 g) finely chopped mint leaves

2 cloves garlic, finely minced

¼ tsp crushed red pepper flakes

Lemon wedges, to serve

Preheat the oven to 450°F (230°C, or gas mark 8).

Place the salmon fillet on a sheet pan lined with parchment paper and pat it dry using a clean paper towel. Brush the melted butter all over the salmon and set it aside.

Now, in a small bowl, stir together the salt, paprika, onion powder, garlic powder and cayenne pepper. Sprinkle the spice mixture over the salmon and use your hands to gently rub the mixture all over the fish. Transfer the sheet pan to the preheated oven and roast for 10 minutes. Turn the oven to broil and continue to cook for about 3 minutes. When done, an instant read thermometer inserted into the thickest part of the fish should read at least 145°F (63°C).

To make the chimichurri sauce, add the lemon juice, olive oil, cilantro, parsley, mint, garlic and crushed red pepper flakes to a small mixing bowl. Whisk to combine. Season the mixture with a little sea salt to taste.

Remove the salmon from the oven and let it cool for about 5 minutes. Serve with the chimichurri and lemon wedges.

GARLIC-BUTTER SPATCHCOCK CHICKEN AND VEGETABLES

SERVES
6

MACROS
Fat: 21.5 g
Carbs: 10.1 g
Net carbs:
6.5 g
Protein: 17.2 g
Fiber: 3.6 g

If you've never spatchcocked, or butterflied, a whole chicken before, you are in for a treat. It has been years since I roasted a chicken without butterflying it. Spatchcocking a whole chicken allows it to cook faster and more evenly and—most important—it ensures the chicken skin gets golden brown and crispy all around. Truly, once you start spatchcocking your bird, you will never go back.

¼ cup (57 g) softened unsalted butter

1 tsp sea salt, plus more as needed

4 cloves garlic, grated

4 lb (1.8 kg) whole chicken

¼ cup (60 ml) avocado oil, divided

1 tsp finely chopped fresh rosemary

Black pepper

1 lb (454 g) Brussels sprouts, cleaned and halved

1 large onion, diced into 1-inch (2.5-cm) pieces

Lemon wedges, to serve

Position the oven rack about 8 inches (20 cm) from the heat source and preheat the oven to 425°F (220°C, or gas mark 7).

Combine the butter, salt and the garlic in a small bowl. Set it aside.

To spatchcock the chicken, place the chicken breast side down on a cutting board with the tail end facing toward you. Use sharp kitchen shears to cut along the right side of the backbone from the tail to the neck. Next, cut along the left side of the backbone as you did on the right side. Remove the backbone and save it for making stock or broth. Flatten the bird by pressing down on each of the wings at the same time until the breastbone cracks. Turn the chicken over so it lays flat.

Use your hands to rub the butter mixture all under the skin of the chicken. Transfer the chicken to a large sheet pan with the bone side up. Combine 2 tablespoons (30 ml) of avocado oil and the rosemary in a small bowl. Brush half of the mixture over the bone side of the chicken and season with a couple pinches of salt and pepper. Flip the chicken so the breast side is up. Brush the remaining avocado oil and rosemary mixture all over the skin of the chicken and season with a couple pinches of salt and pepper. Tuck the wing tips under the chicken so they don't burn.

Transfer the chicken to the oven, breast side up, and roast it for 20 minutes.

While the chicken is in the oven, toss the Brussels sprouts and onion with the remaining 2 tablespoons (30 ml) of avocado oil. Season with a couple pinches of salt and black pepper. After the chicken has roasted for 20 minutes, scatter the Brussels sprouts and onion all around the chicken and continue to cook for about 25 to 30 minutes, until an instant thermometer inserted into the thickest part of the chicken reaches 165°F (74°C).

Allow the chicken to rest for at least 10 to 15 minutes before cutting. Serve with lemon wedges.

MACROS

Fat: 28.5 g

Carbs: 9.7 g

Net carbs:
5.9 g

Protein:
35.8 g

Fiber: 3.8 g

BRUSCHETTA CHICKEN
AND SQUASH

When you think of classic bruschetta, you usually picture vibrant tomatoes served on top of grilled bread of some kind. In this case, I am pairing a light and earthy tomato salad over tender and juicy chicken breasts that are covered with bubbly mozzarella cheese. And the best part is it's all done on one sheet pan so you won't spend any time cleaning up.

1 zucchini

2 yellow squash

4 boneless, skinless chicken breasts

Sea salt and black pepper

¼ cup (60 ml) avocado oil

1 pint (300 g) cherry tomatoes, halved

1 tbsp (15 ml) balsamic vinegar

4 cloves garlic, finely minced

2 tbsp (30 ml) olive oil

8 basil leaves, thinly sliced

3 oz (85 g) fresh mozzarella cheese, sliced into 4 equal slices

Preheat the oven to 375°F (190°C, or gas mark 5). Spray a large sheet pan with avocado oil spray and set it aside.

Cut the zucchini and yellow squash in half lengthwise then slice them into ¼-inch (6-mm) pieces. Transfer the vegetables to one side of the prepared sheet pan and set it aside.

Season the chicken breasts with a couple pinches of salt and pepper on both sides and transfer them to the other side of the sheet pan. Drizzle the avocado oil over the chicken breasts and the vegetables and sprinkle a couple pinches of salt and pepper on top of the zucchini and yellow squash. Transfer the pan to the preheated oven. Roast the chicken and vegetables for 20 minutes.

In the meantime, transfer the cherry tomatoes to a mixing bowl along with the balsamic vinegar, garlic, olive oil and basil leaves. Toss all the ingredients together and season with salt to taste. Set the tomato mixture aside.

Remove the chicken and vegetables from the oven and increase the temperature to 425°F (220°C, or gas mark 7). Add 1 slice of mozzarella cheese on top of each chicken breast. Transfer the pan back into the oven for 5 to 7 minutes, or until the chicken is cooked through and the cheese is melted and bubbling.

Serve the tomato mixture over the chicken.

MINI MEATLOAF DINNER

SERVES
4

MACROS
Fat: 30.8 g
Carbs: 21.3 g
Net carbs:
16 g
Protein:
30.8 g
Fiber: 5.3 g

This is definitely not your grandmother's meatloaf—it is better. No more dry meatloaf here! This one is tender, juicy and packed with loads of flavor. Throw it all on one sheet pan and then into the oven. Before you know it, dinner is ready, cleanup is a breeze and everyone gets their own mini meatloaf.

1 leek

¼ cup (60 ml) avocado oil, divided

1 shallot, minced

4 cloves garlic, finely minced

1 tsp sea salt, plus more to taste

½ tsp black pepper, plus more to taste

2 tbsp (32 g) tomato paste

1 lb (454 g) ground beef

2 eggs

2 tbsp (13 g) almond flour

1 lb (454 g) fresh green beans, cleaned and trimmed

2 red bell peppers, diced

1 large onion, diced

½ cup (120 ml) no-sugar-added ketchup

Chives, to garnish

Preheat the oven to 400°F (200°C, or gas mark 6).

Clean the leek by slicing off the dark green part, trimming to the part where the color is paler. Then, cut off the end and slice it lengthwise. Thinly chop the leek into half-moon slices and submerge them in a bowl of cold water. Gently rub the leeks to remove any soil or dirt.

Heat 2 tablespoons (30 ml) of the avocado oil in a skillet over medium heat. Remove the leeks from the water and add them to the skillet along with the shallot, garlic, salt and pepper. Sauté the vegetables until the leeks are tender, about 5 to 7 minutes. Add the tomato paste and cook for about 2 minutes. Remove the vegetable mixture from the heat and allow it to cool for at least 7 minutes.

Transfer the cooked vegetable mixture to a large mixing bowl along with the ground beef, eggs and almond flour. Use a fork to combine all the ingredients, being careful not to overmix.

Toss the green beans, bell peppers, onion, the remaining 2 tablespoons (30 ml) of avocado oil and a couple pinches of salt and pepper in a bowl.

Cut four 10 x 12-inch (25 x 30-cm) pieces of aluminum foil. Add an equal amount of vegetables to the center of each piece of foil. Bring the long sides of the foil up so the ends meet over the vegetables. Double fold the ends, leaving room for heat circulation, and double fold the two short ends to seal the packet. Place the vegetable packets on one side of a large sheet pan.

Spray the other side of the sheet pan with avocado oil spray. Divide the meat mixture into four equal sections. Mold each section into a 4 x 2½-inch (10 x 6-cm) meatloaf and place each meatloaf on the other side of the sheet pan. Brush each meatloaf with about 2 tablespoons (30 ml) of ketchup. Transfer the pan to the oven and bake for 30 to 35 minutes.

Let the meatloaf rest for about 5 minutes, garnish with chives and serve with the vegetables.

SERVES
4

MACROS
Fat: 31 g
Carbs: 13.8 g
Net carbs:
9.6 g
Protein: 33 g
Fiber: 4.2 g

SALMON NIÇOISE SALAD
WITH MUSTARD DRESSING

Niçoise salad, like most other salads, is very versatile. Although we are using salmon, you can also use tuna, chicken or even steak. The possibilities are endless, so that means it's a great option for feeding a crowd. You can use greens such as arugula and spinach in place of romaine lettuce.

---

1 lb (454 g) fresh green beans, cleaned and trimmed

1 lb (454 g) wild sockeye salmon

Sea salt and black pepper

3 tbsp (45 ml) lemon juice, divided

5 tbsp (75 ml) olive oil, divided

2 tbsp (30 ml) coconut aminos

1 tsp finely chopped fresh rosemary

1 tsp yellow mustard

1 head romaine lettuce, cleaned and chopped

¼ cup (45 g) pitted green olives

¼ cup (45 g) pitted Kalamata olives

4 hard-boiled eggs, halved

Preheat the oven to 450°F (230°C, or gas mark 8). Spray a large sheet pan with avocado oil spray and set it aside.

Place the green beans on a large 12 x 18–inch (30 x 46–cm) piece of aluminum foil and transfer the foil to the sheet pan. Place the salmon fillet skin side down directly onto the sheet pan next to the green beans. Season both the salmon fillet and the green beans with a couple pinches of salt and pepper.

Combine 2 tablespoons (30 ml) of lemon juice, 3 tablespoons (45 ml) of olive oil, the coconut aminos and rosemary in a small bowl. Pour this mixture over the salmon and green beans. Fold one end of the aluminum foil over the green beans and double fold the ends to close the packet.

Transfer the sheet pan to the oven and roast the salmon and green beans for 10 minutes. Remove the sheet pan from the oven. Let the salmon and green beans rest for about 10 minutes.

Make the dressing by combining the remaining 2 tablespoons (30 ml) of olive oil with the mustard and the remaining 1 tablespoon (15 ml) of lemon juice in a bowl. Stir all the ingredients together and set the dressing aside.

To assemble the salad, open the foil packet with the green beans and scatter the beans around the salmon. Use a fork to gently flake the salmon. Scatter the romaine lettuce, olives and hard-boiled eggs around the salmon, and finish by drizzling the dressing all over the salad.

SHEET-PAN KUNG PAO CHICKEN

SERVES
4

MACROS
Fat: 24.9 g
Carbs: 18.1 g
Net carbs: 12.3 g
Protein: 23.6 g
Fiber: 5.8 g

Whenever I think about re-creating a classic takeout dish at home, my main focus is never authenticity. I am more focused on the taste, flavors and textures that bring me joy or that cater to my diet. So, with a dish like kung pao chicken, I simply focused on bringing the Sichuan flavor to ingredients that fit my Keto lifestyle. Of course, as with most of these kinds of recipes, you can switch out the vegetables to your liking.

1 lb (454 g) boneless, skinless chicken thighs, cut into 1-inch (2.5-cm) pieces

1 tbsp (15 ml) sesame oil

1½ tsp (8 ml) rice vinegar, divided

1 tbsp (7 g) coconut flour

3 tbsp (45 ml) coconut aminos, divided

2 tbsp (30 ml) harissa sauce (page 170)

2 tbsp (30 ml) avocado oil

2 Thai chilis, minced

1 head broccoli, cut into florets

1 red bell pepper, diced

1 orange bell pepper, diced

¼ cup (33 g) roasted macadamia nuts, roughly chopped, divided

Sea salt and black pepper

Preheat the broiler to the highest setting. Spray a large sheet pan with avocado oil spray and set it aside.

Toss the chicken with the sesame oil, 1 teaspoon of rice vinegar, coconut flour and 1 tablespoon (15 ml) of coconut aminos. Spread the chicken thighs on the prepared sheet pan in a single layer. Transfer the pan to the oven and cook the chicken for 5 minutes, flipping halfway through.

In the meantime, make the sauce by combining the remaining ½ teaspoon of rice vinegar along with the remaining 2 tablespoons (30 ml) of coconut aminos, the harissa sauce, avocado oil and Thai chilis in a small bowl. Give the sauce a quick stir and set it aside.

Remove the chicken from the oven, pour half of the sauce over the chicken and toss to coat. Then add the broccoli, bell peppers and half of the macadamia nuts to the pan along with the rest of the sauce. Toss the chicken and vegetables together to make sure they are well coated with the sauce. Season with a couple pinches of salt and pepper.

Turn the oven to bake at 425°F (220°C, or gas mark 7). Return the sheet pan to the oven and continue to cook for 15 to 20 minutes, or until the vegetables are al dente. Add the remaining macadamia nuts on top.

MACROS

Fat: 19.4 g

Carbs: 18.6 g

Net carbs:
12.9 g

Protein:
27.6 g

Fiber: 5.7 g

HERB BUTTER COD
AND VEGETABLES

White fish is foolproof to make, and cod in particular is pretty much impossible to mess up: It cooks quickly. It's hard to overcook, unless you really forget about it. And it will absorb any flavor you add to it. A little herb butter and lemon is definitely my favorite way to cook cod. It's simple, easy and bursting with flavor.

½ butternut squash, peeled and diced

1 head broccoli, cut into florets

2 tbsp (30 ml) avocado oil

Sea salt and black pepper

¼ cup (57 g) softened unsalted butter

4 cloves garlic, grated

1 tsp chopped fresh rosemary

1 tbsp (1 g) chopped fresh cilantro leaves

4 boneless, skinless cod fillets

2–4 lemon slices

Preheat the oven to 400°F (200°C, or gas mark 6).

Place the butternut squash and broccoli florets on a large sheet pan lined with parchment paper. Drizzle the avocado oil over the vegetables and season with a couple pinches of salt and pepper. Toss the vegetables and scatter them in a single layer. Roast the vegetables for 15 minutes.

In the meantime, add the butter, garlic, rosemary and cilantro to a bowl and stir to combine.

Season each piece of fish with salt and pepper on both sides and rub about 1 tablespoon (15 ml) of the butter mixture all over each cod fillet.

Remove the vegetables from the oven and push them to one side of the sheet pan. Place the cod fillets on the other side of the sheet pan and add the lemon slices around the fish. Return the pan to the oven and bake until the cod is opaque and flakes easily using a fork, about 12 to 15 minutes.

Allow the fish to cool for a few minutes before serving.

EASY WEEKNIGHT
CARNITAS TACOS

SERVES
6

MACROS
Fat: 13 g
Carbs: 8.2 g
Net carbs:
5.8 g
Protein:
29.6 g
Fiber: 2.4 g

Taco night is no joke in my house, and I have a feeling it is the same for you! Carnitas are pretty much my favorite thing about taco night. The flavor, the crispy bits—it's all just phenomenal. Of course, you can make carnitas in your slow cooker or Instant Pot®, but I prefer it on a sheet pan in the oven. This way, we are able to achieve tender and juicy, yet crispy, carnitas every time!

2 lb (907 g) boneless pork shoulder, cut into 2-inch (5-cm) pieces

1 tsp sea salt

4 cloves garlic, finely minced

½ tsp crushed red pepper flakes

1 tsp chili powder

1 tsp ground cumin

1 tsp black pepper

1 onion, sliced

8 Napa cabbage leaves (romaine lettuce leaves will also work well)

1 avocado, sliced

1 jalapeño pepper, sliced

1 lime, cut into wedges

Salsa of your choice

Preheat the oven to 375°F (190°C, or gas mark 5).

In a large mixing bowl, add the pork shoulder with the salt, garlic, crushed red pepper flakes, chili powder, cumin and black pepper. Use your hands to massage the pork and make sure each piece is well coated with the spices. Transfer the pork to a large sheet pan along with the onion and spread out the pieces in a single layer.

Cover the sheet pan with aluminum foil and transfer the pan to the oven. Roast the pork, covered, for 1½ hours.

After 1½ hours of cooking, remove the pork from the oven and drain off most of the liquid. Use two forks to shred the pork pieces and set the oven to broil on high. Return the pork to the oven, uncovered, for 5 minutes until the edges are brown and crispy.

Serve the pork inside of the cabbage leaves and finish with avocado slices, jalapeños, lime wedges and salsa.

MACROS
Fat: 26.3 g
Carbs: 8.2 g
Net carbs:
4.7 g
Protein:
24.9 g
Fiber: 3.5 g

JUICY GARLIC-BUTTER
PORK CHOP DINNER

Cooking pork chops at home can be a little tricky because it's very easy to overcook them. But my foolproof sheet-pan method of broiling then baking the pork chops leaves them tender and juicy. But the star of this dish is definitely the garlic-butter sauce. It's a little sweet and salty, and it gives this simple dish layers of flavor.

2 tbsp (28 g) butter, melted

1 tbsp (15 ml) coconut aminos

2 cloves garlic, finely minced

1 tbsp (3 g) finely minced fresh thyme

4 pork chops, bone-in and center cut

Sea salt and black pepper

3 tbsp (45 ml) avocado oil, divided

1 (12-oz [340-g]) bag fresh green beans, trimmed

Set the broiler to high.

To make the butter sauce, combine the butter, coconut aminos, garlic and thyme in a small bowl. Set it aside.

Pat the pork chops dry using paper towels. Spray a large sheet pan with avocado oil spray and place the pork chops on the sheet pan. Season the chops with a few pinches of salt and pepper on both sides and brush one side of the chops with 1 tablespoon (15 ml) of avocado oil. Transfer them to the oven and cook the chops under the broiler for 5 minutes.

Remove the chops from the oven and push them to one side of the sheet pan. Turn the oven to bake at 450°F (230°C, or gas mark 8). Place the green beans on the other side of the sheet pan. Drizzle the remaining avocado oil over the beans and season with a couple pinches of salt and pepper. Brush the butter sauce all over the pork chops and return the sheet pan to the oven. Bake for 12 to 15 minutes depending on the thickness of your pork chops. The internal temperature of your pork chops should be 145°F (63°C).

Let the chops rest for about 3 to 5 minutes before serving.

5-INGREDIENT CHICKEN
AND ASPARAGUS

SERVES
4

MACROS
Fat: 22.8 g

Carbs: 4.8 g

Net carbs:
3 g

Protein:
21.7 g

Fiber: 1.8 g

Another five-ingredient meal for the books. This one may seem very simple, but it packs a punch when it comes to flavor. We are pairing salty, nutty Parmesan cheese with juicy chicken thighs and then finishing the meal with the bright, clean and earthy flavor of lightly roasted asparagus. This meal is ready in no time, and it is one you will want to make over and over again.

4 boneless, skinless chicken thighs

Sea salt and black pepper, to taste

Garlic powder, to taste

¼ cup (60 ml) avocado oil, divided

1 bunch thin asparagus

¼ cup (25 g) grated Parmesan cheese

Preheat the oven to 450°F (230°C, or gas mark 8).

Place the chicken thighs on one side of a large sheet pan. Season the chicken thighs with a couple pinches of salt, pepper and garlic powder on both sides and drizzle 2 tablespoons (30 ml) of avocado oil over the chicken. Transfer the pan to the oven and cook for 10 minutes.

To trim the asparagus, cut off about 1½ to 2 inches (3.5 to 5 cm) from the flat ends of the asparagus and set them aside.

Remove the chicken from the oven. Place the asparagus on the other side of the sheet pan and drizzle the remaining 2 tablespoons (30 ml) of avocado oil all over the asparagus. Sprinkle an even amount of Parmesan cheese on top of each chicken thigh.

Return the sheet pan to the oven and cook for 5 to 7 minutes. Serve immediately.

MACROS
Fat: 14.3 g
Carbs: 12.2 g
Net carbs:
7.9 g
Protein: 12 g
Fiber: 4.3 g

SHEET-PAN JAMBALAYA

In my opinion there is nothing more quintessentially Creole than a heavenly bowl of jambalaya. Every layer of this dish is bursting with flavor. The slightly salty bite from the sausage is balanced by the earthiness of the bell peppers, while the warm Cajun spices make the perfect pairing for fresh wild-caught shrimp. It's the perfect warm and cozy meal for any night of the week.

---

6 oz (170 g) no-sugar-added kielbasa sausage, sliced (see Pro Tip)

1 onion, sliced

1 red bell pepper, sliced

2 tbsp (30 ml) avocado oil

2 tsp (5 g) Cajun seasoning, divided

2 tbsp (32 g) tomato paste

2 (12-oz [340-g]) bags frozen cauliflower rice

Sea salt and black pepper

½ lb (226 g) wild-caught shrimp, peeled and deveined with tails on

2 tbsp (30 ml) melted butter

Fresh parsley, to garnish

Preheat the oven to 425°F (220°C, or gas mark 7).

Add the kielbasa sausage, onion and bell pepper to a large sheet pan along with the avocado oil and 1 teaspoon of Cajun seasoning. Toss the vegetables and the sausage to make sure they are well coated. Transfer the pan to the oven and cook for 10 minutes.

Remove the vegetables and sausage from the oven, add the tomato paste and stir to thoroughly mix it in with the vegetables. Add the frozen cauliflower rice and the remaining teaspoon of Cajun seasoning to the pan. Toss all the ingredients together until they are well incorporated and return the pan to the oven. Continue to cook for 15 to 20 minutes, stirring occasionally, until the cauliflower rice is cooked through and most of the liquid has evaporated.

Taste the jambalaya and season with salt and pepper to taste. Add the raw shrimp on top of the jambalaya and drizzle the butter all over the top.

Return the pan to the oven and cook for 5 to 7 minutes, until the shrimp is cooked through and pink. Garnish with fresh parsley.

PRO TIP: For a no-sugar-added kielbasa, I enjoy Pederson's Natural Farms, usually found at Whole Foods and other specialty grocery stores. If you can't find kielbasa, try using no-sugar-added Cajun sausage. I like the one by Aidells, which is usually found in Super Target stores. It might be in grocery stores local to you; use their store locator for more information.

GARLIC-GINGER
CHICKEN WINGS

I know you've been looking for a go-to chicken wings recipe for your next game day party. Of course, I've got you covered! These wings do not take much effort to make, but they are so packed with flavor that you will be patting yourself on the back when you serve these to your friends and family. You can easily double the recipe to feed a crowd.

SERVES
6

MACROS
Fat: 26.6 g
Carbs: 2.5 g
Net carbs: 2.2 g
Protein: 28.1 g
Fiber: 0.3 g

2 lbs (907 g) chicken wings

1 tsp sea salt

½ tsp black pepper

1 tbsp (15 ml) plus 1 tsp sesame oil, divided

3 tbsp (45 ml) coconut aminos

2 tbsp (30 ml) harissa sauce (page 170)

2 cloves garlic, grated

½ tsp crushed red pepper flakes

1 tbsp (6 g) grated ginger

Chopped scallions and sesame seeds, to garnish

Preheat the oven to 425°F (220°C, or gas mark 7). Spray a large sheet pan with avocado oil spray and set it aside.

Toss the chicken wings with sea salt, black pepper and 1 tablespoon (15 ml) of sesame oil. Transfer the wings to the prepared sheet pan and bake the chicken for 20 to 25 minutes. Flip the chicken about halfway through the cooking process.

In the meantime, make the glaze by mixing the remaining 1 teaspoon of sesame oil, coconut aminos, harissa sauce, garlic, crushed red pepper flakes and ginger in a small bowl and stirring to combine.

Remove the chicken from the oven and turn the oven to broil. Pour the glaze over the chicken wings and toss to coat. Again, spread the chicken out in a single layer and return them to the oven. Continue to cook the chicken under the broiler for 5 to 7 minutes.

Garnish with scallions and sesame seeds.

SHEET-PAN SHRIMP SCAMPI

If you are a garlic lover like me, this is going to become one of your favorites. All the buttery garlic flavor of this dish is what makes shrimp scampi so loved. You can enjoy scampi as an appetizer, but I like serving it with something a little more substantial, such as delicata squash, for a more balanced meal. You can also try serving shrimp scampi with zucchini noodles (page 161) or spaghetti squash.

2 delicata squash

¼ cup (60 ml) olive oil, divided

½ tsp sea salt, divided

½ tsp black pepper, divided

2 tbsp (28 g) unsalted butter, melted

4 cloves garlic, finely minced

Zest of 1 lemon, plus lemon wedges, to garnish

¼ tsp crushed red pepper flakes

1 lb (454 g) wild-caught shrimp, peeled and deveined with tails on

Fresh parsley, to garnish

Preheat the oven to 425°F (220°C, or gas mark 7).

Thoroughly wash the squash, making sure you give it a good scrub with a brush. Place one squash on a cutting board and cut off both ends. Cut it down the center lengthwise and scoop out the seeds. Cut the squash into thin ¼-inch (6-mm) half-moon slices. Transfer it to a large sheet pan. Repeat with the second squash. Drizzle 2 tablespoons (30 ml) of olive oil over the squash and season with ¼ teaspoon of salt and ¼ teaspoon of pepper. Roast it for 20 to 25 minutes, or until it is fork tender.

In the meantime, make the scampi sauce by adding the butter, garlic, lemon zest, crushed red pepper flakes, the remaining 2 tablespoons (30 ml) of olive oil and the remaining ¼ teaspoon of both salt and pepper to a small mixing bowl. Stir the mixture to combine and set it aside.

Remove the squash from the oven and increase the oven temperature to 450°F (230°C, or gas mark 8). Gently push the squash to one side of the sheet pan and scatter the shrimp on the other side of the sheet pan. Pour the scampi sauce all over the shrimp and return the sheet pan to the oven. Cook until the shrimp is cooked through and has a gorgeous pink color, about 10 to 12 minutes.

Garnish with lemon wedges and fresh parsley.

GLAZED TERIYAKI SALMON

SERVES
4

MACROS
Fat: 17.6 g
Carbs: 6.8 g
Net carbs:
5 g
Protein:
26.4 g
Fiber: 1.8 g

Salmon is a part of my dinner rotation at least three times a week. So, I really enjoy creating new and fun ways to use it. My friend who made me teriyaki salmon a little while ago definitely inspired this recipe. Shockingly, I had never had teriyaki salmon, but now it is one of my favorite dinners. The sweetness of the sauce paired with the buttery, flaky salmon is truly an experience worth diving into.

¼ cup (60 ml) coconut aminos

1 tsp grated ginger

½ tsp garlic powder

1 tbsp (15 ml) sesame oil

1 tsp Swerve or monk fruit sweetener

½ tsp crushed red pepper flakes

4 salmon fillets

1 bunch asparagus, trimmed

2 tbsp (30 ml) avocado oil

Sea salt and black pepper

Preheat the oven to 425°F (220°C, or gas mark 7).

To make the teriyaki sauce, combine the coconut aminos, ginger, garlic powder, sesame oil, sweetener and crushed red pepper flakes in a large bowl. Stir to combine. Nestle the salmon fillets in the sauce and marinate for 5 to 7 minutes.

Transfer the salmon fillets skin side down to one side of a large sheet pan and brush the remaining marinade on top of the salmon. Add the asparagus to the other side of the sheet pan and drizzle the avocado oil over the asparagus. Season both the asparagus and salmon fillets with a couple pinches of salt and pepper.

Roast the salmon and asparagus for 12 to 15 minutes, or until the asparagus is fork tender and the salmon is flaky. Let the fish rest for a few minutes and serve.

SERVES
4

MACROS
Fat: 24.3 g
Carbs: 9 g
Net carbs:
7.1 g
Protein:
21.4 g
Fiber: 1.9 g

STEAK AND PEPPERS DINNER

My aunt made this steak dinner for me a while back, and I enjoyed it so much that I called her up and asked her what she did. Her answer? "I just threw everything on a sheet pan." As you can imagine, that was not very helpful, but I was able to put my own spin on it for you. It's a very quick and easy dish, and the steak comes out incredibly juicy and tender.

2 red bell peppers, deseeded and sliced into thick rounds

2 large onions, peeled and sliced into thick rounds

2 (12-oz [340-g]) boneless rib eye steaks, room temperature

¼ cup (57 g) butter, melted

2 tbsp (30 ml) olive oil

4 tsp (10 g) steak seasoning, divided

Position the oven rack about 6 inches (15 cm) from the heat source and preheat the broiler to high.

Spread the bell peppers and onions on a large sheet pan. Add the steak on top of the vegetables. Mix the butter and olive oil together in a small bowl. Brush about half of the mixture onto the steaks and season each steak with 1 teaspoon of steak seasoning.

Transfer the sheet pan to the oven and broil for 7 minutes, or until the tops of the steaks are brown and sizzling. Remove the pan from the oven, flip the steaks and repeat the same steps: Brush the remaining butter and oil mixture all over the steaks and season each one with 1 teaspoon of steak seasoning.

Return the sheet pan to the oven and broil for 4 to 5 minutes. Following these instructions will result in medium-rare steak. For medium, cook for an additional 2 to 3 minutes per side. Tent the steaks with foil and allow them to rest for at least 5 minutes. Slice the steaks and serve with the roasted peppers and onions.

STICKY SHEET-PAN
PORK RIBS

SERVES

6

MACROS

Fat: 17.3 g

Carbs: 7.5 g

Net carbs:
7 g

Protein:
40.3 g

Fiber: 0.5 g

I may not be the master of BBQ, but I must admit, these ribs may be coming for all the crowned BBQ kings and queens out there! Now I know the ingredient list may be a little long, but I promise they are all spices you already have in your cabinets. The key to these ribs is patience: They need to be cooked for a couple of hours, but the end result is well worth the wait.

2½ lbs (1.1 kg) pork ribs

1½ tsp (3 g) paprika

1 tsp sea salt

1 tsp black pepper

½ tsp cayenne pepper

1 tsp onion powder

1 tsp garlic powder

¼ tsp ground cumin

2 tbsp (30 ml) olive oil

¼ cup (60 ml) no-sugar-added BBQ sauce

2 tbsp (30 ml) coconut aminos

1 tsp apple cider vinegar

Preheat the oven to 350°F (175°C, or gas mark 4).

Peel off the tough membrane that covers the bone side of the ribs. Place the ribs on a sheet pan lined with aluminum foil.

Combine the paprika, salt, black pepper, cayenne pepper, onion powder, garlic powder and cumin in a bowl. Sprinkle the spice mixture all over both sides of the ribs. Drizzle 1 tablespoon (15 ml) of olive oil on each side and rub the spice mixture all over the ribs. Cover the ribs with foil and roast them for 2 hours.

In the meantime, mix the BBQ sauce, coconut aminos and apple cider vinegar together. Set it aside.

Remove the ribs from the oven, uncover and brush the BBQ sauce mixture all over the ribs. Turn the oven to broil and return the ribs to the oven, uncovered. Broil for 5 to 7 minutes.

Remove the ribs from the oven and let them rest for 7 to 10 minutes before serving.

OVEN TO TABLE

WHENEVER I THINK OF ONE-POT MEALS, it brings me right back to my childhood. My grandmother and I were always experimenting with different casseroles, braising methods or anything we could cook just by throwing something into the oven and calling it a day. So, my love for decadent baked dishes has been brewing for a very long time.

This chapter excites me in a very special way because it really is a nod to my grandmother. I had to include some of her classics, such as Grandma Toulia's Ratatouille (page 84) and Incredible Eggplant Parmesan (page 99). But there are also easy "dump and go" recipes that require less prep work, such as Date Night Salsa Verde Chicken Bake (page 88) and Classic Meatballs in Spicy Tomato Sauce (page 104).

You will find we use a few different baking methods in this collection of recipes. Some, such as Spaghetti Squash Parmesan (page 108), are twice baked, while other dishes, such as Mexican Stuffed Peppers (page 96), are finished in the oven. No matter the method, they are all warm and welcoming meals that will only spark joy.

MACROS
Fat: 9.6 g
Carbs: 16 g
Net carbs:
11.2 g
Protein: 4.3 g
Fiber: 4.8 g

GRANDMA TOULIA'S
RATATOUILLE

This dish is almost too beautiful to eat. My grandmother taught me how to make ratatouille, and it has become a staple for me whenever I entertain. Put this beauty on the dinner table and your friends and family will think you spent all day making it.

2 zucchinis

2 yellow squash

2 Chinese eggplant

¼ cup (60 ml) olive oil, divided

1 onion, diced

2 cloves garlic, finely minced

Sea salt and black pepper

1 (28-oz [794-g]) can crushed tomatoes

2 tbsp (30 ml) harissa sauce (page 170) or garlic chili paste

1 tbsp (3 g) finely chopped fresh thyme

1 tbsp (3 g) chopped fresh basil, to garnish

Preheat the oven to 375°F (190°C, or gas mark 5).

Thoroughly wash the zucchinis, yellow squash and eggplant and wipe them dry. Use a sharp knife to slice them into approximately ¹⁄₁₆-inch (1.6-mm) rounds. Set them aside.

To make the sauce, heat 2 tablespoons (30 ml) of olive oil in a 12-inch (30-cm) cast-iron or oven-safe skillet over medium-high heat. Add the onion and garlic and sauté for 5 to 7 minutes, or until the onion is tender. Season with salt and pepper and add the tomatoes, harissa sauce and thyme to the pan.

Stir the sauce to combine all the ingredients and simmer for 7 to 10 minutes to thicken the sauce. Turn the heat off and begin adding the vegetables.

Arrange the vegetables in an alternating pattern—zucchini, eggplant, yellow squash—on top of the sauce from the outer edge of the pan toward the center. Drizzle the remaining 2 tablespoons (30 ml) of olive oil on top of the vegetables and season with salt and pepper.

Bake the ratatouille for 40 to 45 minutes, or until the tomato sauce is bubbling and the vegetables are tender. Garnish with fresh basil.

PRO TIP: If you can't find Chinese eggplant, use Italian eggplant. They are the fat ones commonly found in most grocery stores. Just make sure you cut them to roughly the same size as the zucchini and yellow squash. You may have to cut them in half or into quarters.

HERB ZUCCHINI GRATIN

SERVES
4

MACROS
Fat: 28.8 g
Carbs: 9.3 g
Net carbs:
8 g
Protein:
6.6 g
Fiber: 1.3 g

Zucchini is always easy to find and it is definitely one of my go-to vegetables while I am on the Keto diet. They are easy to work with and, of course, low-carb. Gratin is usually made with potatoes, which are not an option in the Keto diet. Using zucchini with all the classic flavors of gratin gives us a low-carb, but still decadent, dish.

2 large zucchinis

1 tsp sea salt

3 slices no-sugar-added bacon

1 tbsp (14 g) unsalted butter

2 cloves garlic, finely minced

1 tbsp (7 g) almond flour

½ tsp black pepper

1 cup (240 ml) heavy cream

½ cup (50 g) grated Parmesan cheese

Fresh parsley, to garnish

Preheat the oven to 350°F (175°C, or gas mark 4).

Cut off the ends of each zucchini and slice them into thin, ¼-inch (6-mm) rounds. Lay the zucchini slices in a single layer on top of a few clean sheets of paper towel and sprinkle with the salt. Let the zucchini sit with the salt for 10 to 12 minutes to allow most of the liquid to drain out.

In a 10-inch (25-cm) oven-safe skillet over medium-high heat, crisp the bacon, remove it from the pan and set it aside to cool.

To make the sauce, discard half of the bacon grease (or save it to use another time). Add the butter to the same skillet with the remaining bacon grease. When the butter is melted, add the garlic and sauté it for about 1 minute, until the garlic is fragrant. While stirring, add in the almond flour and black pepper and continue to sauté for 2 minutes. Slowly stir in the heavy cream and bring the sauce to a low simmer.

Use more clean paper towels to pat the zucchini slices and remove all the excess liquid. Arrange the zucchini on top of the sauce from the outer edge to the middle of the pan. Transfer the pan to the oven and bake for 15 minutes.

Crumble the bacon on top of the layered zucchini and top it with the Parmesan cheese. Turn the oven to broil and continue to cook for 2 to 3 minutes to melt the cheese. Garnish with parsley and serve.

MACROS

Fat: 23.8 g

Carbs: 19.3 g

Net carbs:
11.9 g

Protein:
44.9 g

Fiber: 7.4 g

DATE NIGHT SALSA VERDE
CHICKEN BAKE

So, it's date night. You just got home from a long day at work and the last thing you want to do is spend hours in the kitchen. That's where this ultimate "dump and go" salsa verde chicken steps in to save the day! All you need to do is pick out a pretty baking dish, add a few simple ingredients and throw it in the oven. By the time you are done showering and setting the table, dinner is ready to enjoy.

½ lb (226 g) asparagus

1 onion, sliced

2 tbsp (30 ml) avocado oil

2 boneless, skinless chicken breasts

Sea salt and black pepper

¼ tsp ground cumin

½ tsp garlic powder

1 cup (240 ml) jarred salsa verde sauce (see Note)

½ cup (56 g) grated mozzarella cheese

Fresh cilantro leaves, to garnish

Preheat the oven to 350°F (175°C, or gas mark 4).

To trim the asparagus, cut off 2 inches (5 cm) of the flat end of the asparagus and discard.

Divide the asparagus and onion into two equal portions and transfer each portion to a 7-inch (18-cm) oval baking dish. Drizzle 1 tablespoon (15 ml) of avocado oil over the vegetables in each dish and set them aside.

Pat the chicken breasts dry using a clean paper towel. Season each breast with a couple pinches of salt and pepper on both sides. Add one chicken breast directly on top of the asparagus and onion in each baking dish. Sprinkle the cumin and garlic powder on top of each chicken breast and pour an equal amount of salsa verde sauce over each chicken breast.

Cover both pans with aluminum foil and transfer them to a large sheet pan. Transfer the sheet pan to the oven and bake for 25 to 30 minutes, until the vegetables are tender and the chicken is cooked through.

Uncover, add an equal amount of mozzarella cheese on top of each chicken breast and turn the oven to broil. Return the pans to the oven and broil for 3 to 5 minutes, or until the cheese is completely melted. Garnish with fresh cilantro.

NOTE: Double check the ingredient list on your jar of salsa verde and make sure all the ingredients are Keto-friendly. Look for brands that DO NOT include cornstarch and sugar. I like Herdez and Pace brands' salsa verde sauce.

SPAGHETTI SQUASH AND SHRIMP BAKE

SERVES
4

MACROS
Fat: 22.8 g
Carbs: 7.9 g
Net carbs: 7 g
Protein: 22.5 g
Fiber: 0.9 g

Choosing a low-carb lifestyle does not mean we have to miss out on comfort food. This dish is the perfect example of that. All the buttery, warm and delicious flavors of shrimp scampi are paired with tender spaghetti squash noodles. You can also substitute zucchini noodles (page 161).

1 medium spaghetti squash

2 tbsp (30 ml) avocado oil

1 lb (454 g) large shrimp in the shell

¼ tsp sea salt

¼ tsp black pepper

½ tsp lemon zest, plus lemon wedges to serve

¼ cup (60 ml) melted organic grass-fed ghee

2 tbsp (30 ml) lemon juice

½ tsp crushed red pepper flakes

2 cloves garlic, finely minced

1 cup (100 g) grated Parmesan cheese

2 tsp (2 g) chopped fresh parsley

Preheat the oven to 400°F (200°C, or gas mark 6).

Cut the spaghetti squash in half lengthwise and use a spoon to scoop out all the seeds. Rub the inside of each half of the squash with the avocado oil and place the halves in a deep, oven-safe 12-inch (30-cm) skillet or a 9 x 7-inch (23 x 18–cm) casserole dish. Roast the squash for 40 to 45 minutes, or until it is fork tender. Use a fork to pull the strands of noodles away from the spaghetti squash rind. Scatter the spaghetti squash on the bottom of the skillet or a casserole dish and set it aside.

To prepare the shrimp, peel, devein and butterfly the shrimp, leaving the tail on. Toss the shrimp with the salt, pepper and lemon zest. Set it aside.

To prepare the butter sauce, add the ghee, lemon juice, crushed red pepper flakes and garlic to a small bowl. Whisk to combine.

To prepare the crust, toss together the Parmesan cheese and the parsley. Set it aside.

Arrange the shrimp on top of the spaghetti squash in a single layer, cut side down with the tail pointing up and toward the center of the dish. Pour the butter sauce all over the shrimp. Transfer the baking dish to the oven and bake for 15 minutes, or until the shrimp is pink and cooked through.

Remove the dish from the oven and turn the oven to broil. Scatter the Parmesan cheese and parsley crust on top of the shrimp and return the dish to the oven. Broil for 2 to 3 minutes to melt the cheese. Let the dish rest for 5 minutes before serving.

SERVES
4

MACROS
Fat: 13.2 g

Carbs: 4.5 g

Net carbs: 3.7 g

Protein: 16.9 g

Fiber: 0.8 g

BRAISED MUSHROOM
SHORT RIBS

Whenever I think of braised short ribs, I always think elegance and class. But I guess that feeling comes with any great cut of beef, right? Am I alone here? Anyway, as elegant as this dish may seem, it is also extremely easy to put together. The rich and beefy flavor of the short ribs paired with the earthiness of the mushrooms is the combination you didn't know you needed in your life.

½ oz (14 g) dried porcini mushrooms

2 lbs (907 g) bone-in beef short ribs

Sea salt and black pepper

2 tbsp (26 g) organic grass-fed ghee

1 onion, diced

4 cloves garlic, minced

1 tbsp (16 g) tomato paste

2 cups (480 ml) unsalted beef broth

8 oz (226 g) portobello mushrooms

1 bay leaf

Preheat the oven to 350°F (175°C, or gas mark 4).

Soak the porcini mushrooms in warm water for about 15 to 20 minutes. Save about ⅓ cup (80 ml) of the water from the mushrooms and discard the rest. Use your hands to squeeze the excess liquid out of the rehydrated mushrooms, cut the larger pieces into two and set them aside.

Pat the short ribs dry and season with salt and pepper on both sides.

Heat the ghee in a large Dutch oven over medium-high heat and sear the ribs for 3 to 5 minutes on all sides. Remove the ribs from the pan and set them aside. Add the onion and garlic and sauté for about 3 to 5 minutes. Add the tomato paste to the pot. Stir and cook for 1 to 2 minutes. Deglaze the pan by adding the broth along with the liquid you saved from the mushrooms. Stir and lift up all the brown bits from the bottom of the pan.

Return the ribs to the pot and nestle them in the sauce along with the porcini and portobello mushrooms and bay leaf. Stir all the ingredients to combine and transfer the pot to the oven. Cook for 2 hours, or until the ribs are tender and falling off the bone, stirring about halfway through cooking. Remove the ribs from the oven and skim off any extra fat from the top of the sauce.

Discard the bay leaf and transfer the ribs to a serving dish. Season the sauce with salt and pepper to taste. Allow the ribs to cool for about 5 minutes and serve with the sauce.

ZUCCHINI LASAGNA
ROLL-UPS

Another reason to love zucchini: We get to enjoy lasagna the low-carb way. But this is not your ordinary lasagna. These delectable rolls of cheesy goodness are packed with all the flavors of a traditional lasagna without any of the guilt. To make the dish a little heartier, I decided to bake the zucchini rolls in Bolognese sauce, but you can simply use a jar of your favorite marinara.

SERVES

6

MACROS

Fat: 17.4 g

Carbs: 11 g

Net carbs: 8.7 g

Protein: 19 g

Fiber: 2.3 g

3 large zucchinis

½ tsp plus ¼ tsp sea salt, divided

1 cup (246 g) full-fat ricotta cheese

½ cup (50 g) grated Parmesan cheese

1 egg

2 tbsp (8 g) chopped fresh parsley

½ lb (226 g) ground beef

1 shallot, finely diced

2 cloves garlic, finely minced

1 tsp Italian seasoning

2 cups (480 ml) no-sugar-added marinara or arrabbiata sauce (page 162)

1½ cups (168 g) grated mozzarella cheese

Fresh basil, to serve

Preheat the oven to 425°F (220°C, or gas mark 7).

Use a knife or mandoline to slice the zucchini lengthwise into ⅛-inch (3-mm) slices. This should make about 22 to 24 slices. Lay the zucchini slices out on sheets of paper towels in a single layer. Sprinkle with ½ teaspoon of salt and let it sit for 10 to 15 minutes.

Stir the ricotta cheese, Parmesan cheese, egg and parsley together in a bowl.

Heat a large, oven-safe skillet over medium-high heat and brown the ground beef until it's no longer pink, about 5 to 7 minutes. Add the shallot and garlic and continue to cook for 5 minutes. Add the Italian seasoning and marinara sauce to the pan. Stir to combine all the ingredients and remove the sauce from the heat.

Use more sheets of paper towels and pat the zucchini slices to get rid of any excess liquid. Place 1 teaspoon of the cheese mixture along each zucchini slice, roll it up and nestle the zucchini rolls into the skillet with the meat sauce. Repeat with the rest of the zucchini. Sprinkle the mozzarella cheese over the top of the zucchini rolls and transfer the skillet to the oven. Bake for 15 to 20 minutes. Allow to cool for about 5 minutes and serve with fresh basil.

MEXICAN STUFFED PEPPERS

With the mild flavor of nutritious bell peppers as the base of this dish, the possibilities are endless when it comes to the filling. Whatever flavor combination you choose, the filling usually includes meat, vegetables, cheese, rice and sauce. My favorite thing about this dish is it allows you to be as creative as you want to be. So branch off of this recipe and try your own filling combinations.

---

1 lb (454 g) ground beef

1 onion, diced

2 carrots, peeled and diced

2 cloves garlic, finely minced

1 tbsp (8 g) taco seasoning

1 cup (180 g) fire-roasted diced tomatoes

Sea salt and black pepper

6 bell peppers, assorted colors

1 cup (240 ml) beef broth

Sliced jalapeño pepper (optional)

1 cup (116 g) shredded Mexican cheese blend

Preheat the oven to 375°F (190°C, or gas mark 5).

Crumble the ground beef in a large skillet. Cook the beef over medium-high heat for 5 to 7 minutes until it is brown, then drain. Add the onion, carrots and garlic to the skillet and continue to cook until the carrots are tender, 5 to 7 minutes. Stir in the taco seasoning and tomatoes. Let the mixture simmer for 5 minutes, stirring occasionally. Season the mixture with salt and pepper to taste.

Cut the tops off of the bell peppers and remove the seeds. Fill each pepper with an equal amount of the ground beef filling. Place the peppers in the same skillet standing up and pour the broth in the bottom of the pan. Cover the peppers with foil and transfer the skillet to the oven. Cook the peppers for 30 minutes.

Uncover the peppers and add an equal amount of jalapeño slices (if using) and cheese on top of each pepper. Turn the oven to broil and return the skillet to the oven, uncovered. Broil for 3 to 5 minutes, until the cheese is melted and bubbly. Allow the peppers to cool for a few minutes before serving.

INCREDIBLE EGGPLANT
PARMESAN

SERVES
4

MACROS
Fat: 21.2 g
Carbs: 14.2 g
Net carbs:
9.4 g
Protein:
16.4 g
Fiber: 4.8 g

The crème de la crème of Italian comfort food, eggplant Parmesan is a dish you have to try at least once in your lifetime. My one nonnegotiable when it comes to eggplant Parmesan is the eggplant has to have a good crispy crust. To achieve this, I coat the eggplant with equal parts almond flour and Parmesan cheese, then I bake the entire dish on a large sheet pan. Every bite is an experience you will never forget.

1 large eggplant

2 eggs

½ cup (50 g) grated Parmesan cheese

½ cup (52 g) almond flour

1 tbsp (7 g) Italian seasoning

2 cups (480 ml) jarred no-sugar-added marinara

1 cup (112 g) grated mozzarella cheese

Fresh basil, to serve

Preheat the oven to 425°F (220°C, or gas mark 7). Spray a large sheet pan with avocado oil spray and set it aside.

Cut off the ends of the eggplant and cut it into ¼-inch (6-mm) slices.

Beat the eggs in a shallow bowl and set it aside.

Combine the Parmesan cheese, almond flour and Italian seasoning in another shallow bowl and set it aside.

Dip each eggplant slice in the egg and then the Parmesan cheese mixture. Transfer the coated eggplant slices to the prepared sheet pan in a single layer, about ½ inch (1 cm) apart. Use two sheet pans if you do not have one large enough to fit all the eggplant slices.

Bake the eggplant for 20 minutes, flipping them halfway through.

Remove the eggplant from the oven. Add 2 tablespoons (30 ml) of marinara sauce on top of each eggplant slice and add an equal amount of mozzarella cheese on top of the sauce.

Return the pan to the oven and continue to bake for 5 to 7 minutes, or until the cheese is melted and the crust is golden brown. Serve with fresh basil.

SUPREME ZUCCHINI
PIZZA BOATS

Pizza without all the guilt is pretty much at the top of everyone's wish list, right? Well, I've got you covered! What I love about this dish is the versatility. You can switch up the toppings and make it your own—but I have a feeling you will love our quick-and-easy homemade sausage paired with all our favorite pizza toppings.

---

2 large zucchinis

½ lb (226 g) ground pork

¼ tsp sea salt

¼ tsp black pepper

½ tsp fennel seeds

½ tsp Italian seasoning

½ tsp crushed red pepper flakes

1 small bell pepper, diced

3½ oz (100 g) portobello mushrooms, diced

1 tsp coconut aminos

1 cup (240 ml) no-sugar-added marinara or pizza sauce

1 cup (116 g) shredded Mexican cheese blend

¼ red onion, diced

Chopped basil leaves, to garnish

Preheat the oven to 450°F (230°C, or gas mark 8).

Cut the zucchinis in half lengthwise and scoop out the flesh. Save the flesh to add to soup or chop it up very small and add it to a meatloaf mixture (page 57).

Add the ground pork, salt, black pepper, fennel seeds, Italian seasoning and red pepper flakes to a bowl. Mix all the ingredients together to combine. Heat a large, oven-safe skillet over medium-high heat and add the pork mixture. Break up the pork and cook for about 7 minutes, or until it starts to develop some color.

Add the bell pepper, mushrooms and coconut aminos to the pan with the pork. Stir and sauté for 3 to 5 minutes just to warm the vegetables through. You don't want to cook them completely.

Assemble the zucchini boats. Spread an equal amount of marinara sauce in the bottoms of the zucchini boats. Then add an equal amount of the pork and veggie mixture. Finish with an equal amount of cheese and red onion on top. Place each zucchini boat in the same skillet you cooked the pork in. Transfer the skillet to the oven and bake for 12 to 15 minutes, or until the cheese is melted. Garnish with basil leaves and serve.

NOT SO OLD-FASHIONED
BRAISED CABBAGE ROLLS

SERVES
6

MACROS

Fat: 20.9 g

Carbs: 10.4 g

Net carbs: 7.3 g

Protein: 17.9 g

Fiber: 3.1 g

Inexpensive ingredients come together to make an incredible meal. What could be better than that? Cabbage rolls are easy to make and completely customizable. Kids love them, too! Apart from the initial prep work, this is the ultimate one-pot meal. All you need is a little patience to create this mouthwatering meal.

1 head cabbage

1 (10-oz [283-g]) bag frozen cauliflower rice, thawed

½ lb (226 g) ground beef

½ lb (226 g) ground pork

1 small shallot, finely diced

2 cloves garlic, finely minced

1 egg

1 tbsp (4 g) chopped fresh parsley, plus more to garnish

2 tbsp (32 g) tomato paste

1 tsp sea salt

½ tsp black pepper

1 (24-oz [640-ml]) jar arrabbiata sauce or 24 oz (640 ml) homemade arrabbiata (page 162)

Preheat the oven to 350°F (175°C, or gas mark 4).

Boil water in a large Dutch oven. Cut the core out of the cabbage and add it to the boiling water, core side down. Cook the cabbage just until the leaves start to pull away from the head. Set aside 12 leaves for the rolls. Discard the water and save the rest of the cabbage for soup (page 124).

Put the thawed cauliflower rice in cheesecloth and squeeze out all the excess liquid. Add the cauliflower rice along with the ground beef, ground pork, shallot, garlic, egg, parsley, tomato paste, salt and pepper to a mixing bowl. Use your hands or a fork to combine the ingredients. Do not overmix.

Pour the arrabbiata sauce into a 9 x 13–inch (23 x 33–cm) casserole dish and set it aside.

Cut the thick vein from the bottom of each cabbage leaf, making a V-shaped cut. Add a ¼-cup (60-ml) scoop of the meat mixture to a cabbage leaf, overlap the cut ends, fold in the sides and roll up beginning from the cut end. Nestle the cabbage roll, seam side down, into the sauce. Repeat with the rest of the cabbage leaves.

When all of the rolls are made, cover the pan with foil and transfer it to the oven. Bake for 1 hour until the cabbage rolls are tender.

Let the cabbage rolls rest for 5 to 7 minutes before serving with more parsley.

CLASSIC MEATBALLS IN
SPICY TOMATO SAUCE

What could be better than tender and juicy meatballs? How about tender and juicy meatballs slow cooked in a rich and spicy tomato sauce? It's one of those recipes where every ingredient plays a part in making it special. The sauce gets richer as it cooks with the meatballs, and the meatballs get better as they cook in the sauce. Serve over zucchini noodles (page 161).

---

1 lb (454 g) ground beef

1 egg

2 tbsp (13 g) almond flour

¼ cup (25 g) grated Parmesan cheese

4 cloves garlic, finely minced, divided

½ large onion, grated

1 tsp sea salt, plus more to taste

½ tsp black pepper, plus more to taste

2 tbsp (8 g) chopped fresh parsley

2 tbsp (30 ml) avocado oil

1 tsp crushed red pepper flakes

1 (28-oz [794-g]) can fire-roasted crushed tomatoes

2 tbsp (5 g) chopped fresh basil leaves, divided

Add the ground beef, egg, almond flour, Parmesan cheese, half of the garlic, onion, salt, pepper and parsley to a large mixing bowl. Use your hands to combine all the ingredients. Do not overmix. Use a cookie scoop to measure out equal amounts of the meat mixture, form them into balls and transfer them to a tray. You should get 12 to 16 meatballs.

Preheat the oven to 325°F (170°C, or gas mark 3).

Heat a large Dutch oven or oven-safe pot over medium-high heat and add the avocado oil. Once the oil is hot, sear the meatballs for 2 to 3 minutes on all sides until they are brown. Sear the meatballs in batches if your pan is not large enough to hold them all at once. Remove the meatballs from the pan and set them aside.

Add the remaining garlic and the crushed red pepper flakes to the same pan and sauté for 1 minute, or until the garlic is fragrant. Immediately add the tomatoes to the pan and stir to scrape up all the brown bits from the bottom of the pan. Stir in half of the basil leaves and return the meatballs to the pot. Nestle the meatballs into the sauce; it's okay if they are not submerged in the sauce.

Cover the pot, transfer it to the preheated oven and cook for 90 minutes. Remove the meatballs from the oven and let them rest for at least 5 minutes. Uncover the pot, taste the sauce and season with salt and pepper if necessary. Garnish the meatballs with the remaining basil leaves.

HARISSA CHICKEN DINNER

SERVES
4

MACROS
Fat: 16.3 g
Carbs: 16.2 g
Net carbs: 10.5 g
Protein: 24.1 g
Fiber: 5.7 g

I'm sure by now you know how much I love harissa paste and sauce (page 170). So, it's no surprise that it is the main component of this incredibly easy one-skillet dish. Harissa paste is very similar to the chili garlic paste "sambal" and they can easily work as substitutes for one another. Harissa tends to be a little earthier in flavor because it includes spices such as cumin and coriander. If you can't find or make harissa paste, you can use harissa sauce, which is definitely easier to find in most grocery stores and online.

¼ cup (60 ml) harissa sauce (page 170)

2 tsp (10 ml) coconut aminos

1 onion, cubed

1 red bell pepper, deseeded and diced

1 (12-oz [340-g]) bag Brussels sprouts, halved

1 lb (454 g) bone-in, skin-on chicken thighs, extra fat trimmed

Sea salt and black pepper

2 tbsp (30 ml) avocado oil

Lemon wedges and mint leaves, to serve

Preheat the oven to 400°F (200°C, or gas mark 6).

Mix the harissa and coconut aminos together in a small bowl. Set it aside.

Add the onion, bell pepper and Brussels sprouts to a large cast-iron pan. Rub the harissa mixture all over the chicken thighs and nestle them in the same pan with the vegetables. Sprinkle a few pinches of salt and pepper over the chicken and vegetables. Drizzle the avocado oil on top.

Transfer the skillet to the oven and roast the chicken and vegetables for 40 to 45 minutes, or until the chicken is cooked through and the vegetables are tender.

Serve with lemon wedges and fresh mint leaves.

MACROS
Fat: 26.1 g
Carbs: 13.1 g
Net carbs:
10.8 g
Protein: 14 g
Fiber: 2.3 g

SPAGHETTI SQUASH
PARMESAN

Personally, I really enjoy a good meatless meal every now and again—but it has to be so good that I don't miss the meat. If you couldn't already tell, I need to savor each and every one of my meals. So, when I choose to have a meatless meal, it has to be scrumptious. This isn't just any spaghetti squash bake; this one packs a punch in the flavor department. Trust me, you will not miss the meat.

½ oz (14 g) dried shiitake mushrooms

2 small spaghetti squash

2 cloves garlic, grated

2 tbsp (30 ml) olive oil

Sea salt and black pepper

2 cups (480 ml) no-sugar-added marinara sauce

1 (8-oz [226-g]) ball fresh mozzarella cheese, sliced into 8 pieces

1 tsp crushed red pepper flakes

¼ cup (25 g) shaved Parmesan cheese, to garnish

Fresh basil, to garnish

Preheat the oven to 400°F (200°C, or gas mark 6). Line a sheet pan with parchment paper.

Add the dried mushrooms to a bowl with warm water. Set it aside to rehydrate for about 15 to 30 minutes.

Cut both squash in half and remove the seeds. Rub the garlic all over the insides of the squash halves. Rub an equal amount of olive oil all over the insides of the squash and season with a couple pinches of salt and pepper. Place each squash half cut side down on the sheet pan. Roast the squash for 35 to 40 minutes, until the skin is fork tender.

While the squash bakes, chop the rehydrated mushrooms into bite-size pieces and set them aside.

Remove the squash from the oven and flip, flesh side up. Use a fork to scrape most of the squash strings away from the peel.

Turn the oven to 425°F (220°C, or gas mark 7). Fill each squash with about ½ cup (120 ml) of marinara, then add a few pieces of mushroom and finish with 2 slices of mozzarella cheese on top. Sprinkle the crushed red pepper flakes on top and return the squash to the oven. Bake for 15 to 18 minutes, until the cheese is bubbly and golden.

Garnish with shaved Parmesan cheese and fresh basil.

EASY CHICKEN
ENCHILADA SKILLET

My first job ever was working at a small Mexican restaurant in Minneapolis while I was in college, and I fell in love with the food. We didn't eat much takeout growing up, so it was a whole new tasty world for me. One of my favorite things on the menu was chicken enchiladas: the sauce, the tender chicken, the cheese! This is actually the first dish that came to mind when I was thinking up recipes for this book. It took a few tries, but this final version is definitely where it's at!

SERVES
4

MACROS
Fat: 23.6 g
Carbs: 7.4 g
Net carbs:
6.1 g
Protein:
19.2 g
Fiber: 1.3 g

1 tbsp (15 ml) olive oil

1 tbsp (14 g) unsalted butter

1 shallot, finely chopped

½ red bell pepper, diced

2 cloves garlic, finely minced

2 tbsp (32 g) tomato paste

3 tbsp (45 ml) Chicken Bone Broth (page 166) or store-bought

1 tsp chili powder

½ tsp ground cumin

½ tsp cayenne pepper, or less to taste

¼ cup (60 ml) sour cream

1½ cups (210 g) shredded rotisserie chicken

1 cup (116 g) shredded Mexican cheese blend

Fresh cilantro leaves, to garnish

Sliced jalapeños, to garnish (optional)

Cauliflower rice (page 154), to serve

Turn the oven to broil on the highest setting.

Heat the olive oil and butter in an oven-safe skillet over medium-high heat. Add the shallot, bell pepper and garlic to the pan and sauté for 5 to 7 minutes, until the bell pepper is tender. Stir in the tomato paste and cook for about 1 minute. Lower the heat to medium and stir in the broth to deglaze the pan. Stir in the chili powder, cumin and cayenne pepper.

Add the sour cream and stir to combine. Add the chicken and stir to make sure it is well incorporated. Sprinkle the cheese on top and transfer the skillet to the oven. Broil until the cheese is golden and bubbly, about 3 minutes.

Garnish with cilantro and jalapeños (if using), and serve with cauliflower rice.

IRRESISTIBLE GREEN BEAN
CASSEROLE

We never had green bean casserole on our Thanksgiving table growing up, but it's made its way into my holiday traditions. My version is not completely "traditional," but it is incredibly tasty. Although this dish makes for a phenomenal side dish during the holidays, it is also great all year round. I like using fresh green beans for my casserole, but you can certainly use canned or frozen beans.

1 lb (454 g) fresh green beans, trimmed and cut in half

3 slices no-sugar-added bacon

1 tbsp (13 g) organic grass-fed ghee

1 onion, sliced

2 cloves garlic, finely minced

8 oz (226 g) portobello mushrooms, sliced

1 tsp coconut flour

1 tbsp (15 ml) coconut aminos

¾ cup (180 ml) Chicken Bone Broth (page 166) or store-bought

½ cup (120 ml) heavy cream

Sea salt and black pepper

¼ tsp cayenne pepper

½ cup (56 g) grated mozzarella cheese

½ cup (50 g) grated Parmesan cheese

Fresh parsley, to garnish

Preheat the oven to 400°F (200°C, or gas mark 6).

Blanch the green beans. Bring salted water to a boil in a large, deep oven-safe skillet. Prepare an ice bath of half cold water and half ice. Add the green beans to the boiling water. Cook until the beans are bright green but still have some crunch, about 5 minutes. Immediately transfer the cooked beans to the ice bath and set them aside.

Discard the salted water from the skillet and return the skillet to the heat. Add the bacon to the pan and cook over medium-high heat for 2 to 3 minutes per side, turning frequently, until the bacon is crisp. Remove the bacon from the pan and set it aside.

To make the sauce, get rid of about half of the bacon fat, leaving 1 tablespoon (15 ml) in the pan. Add the ghee to the same pan. Sauté the onion until tender, about 3 minutes. Add the garlic and mushrooms and continue to cook the vegetables until the mushrooms are tender, about 5 minutes. Add the coconut flour, stir and cook for about 2 minutes. Add the coconut aminos and broth. Stir to lift all the brown bits from the bottom of the pan. Let the sauce simmer for a few minutes. When it starts to thicken, slowly add the heavy cream and stir to combine. Season with a couple pinches of salt and pepper to taste.

Return the green beans to the pan along with the cayenne pepper and toss to coat the beans with the sauce. Cover the skillet with foil and transfer it to the oven. Bake for 15 to 20 minutes.

Uncover the skillet and add the mozzarella and Parmesan cheese on top. Crumble the bacon on top of the cheese. Turn the oven to broil and return the skillet to the oven. Continue to cook for 3 to 5 minutes, until the cheese is melted and bubbly. Garnish with fresh parsley.

COMFORTING SOUPS AND STEWS

WHETHER IT IS COLD OUTSIDE or it is a lovely summer day, a warm, comforting bowl of your favorite soup or stew makes you feel right at home. And, most importantly, this collection of recipes will help get you through your busiest of days. Instant Pot Chicken Noodle Soup (page 119) and Feel-Good Cabbage Soup (page 124) are just a few examples of recipes that are perfect to make ahead and pair with simple sides.

But this chapter is more than just your meal prep go-to. It's also filled with fun twists on classic dishes such as my Creamy Chicken Potpie Soup (page 123) and Hearty Keto Zuppa Toscana (page 120). These are two favorites that you can put together in under an hour for a warm and cozy dinner the whole family will love on a cold night.

I also want to show you a few different cooking methods in this chapter. I use the slow cooker or Instant Pot in a couple of recipes. I am also sharing a few different techniques such as braising and slow simmering. Some of these dishes do require a little patience, but they are all comforting recipes that are going to become staples in your Keto lifestyle.

MACROS
Fat: 18.4 g
Carbs: 5.8 g
Net carbs:
4 g
Protein:
14.7 g
Fiber: 1.8 g

VINEGAR CHICKEN STEW

This is definitely one for the books. It's a timeless play on classic French cuisine without any of the work. One of my absolute favorite bloggers, Alexandra Stafford over at alexandracooks.com, inspired this recipe. I saw her make a vinegar chicken in a video, and I couldn't get it out of my head. I decided to try my hand at it and the end result will blow your mind and your taste buds.

---

2 tbsp (30 ml) avocado oil

1 lb (454 g) bone-in, skin-on chicken thighs

Sea salt and black pepper

1 onion, diced

2 cloves garlic, finely minced

¼ cup (60 ml) red wine vinegar

1 (14.5-oz [411-g]) can fire-roasted diced tomatoes

1 bay leaf

1 rosemary sprig

Preheat the oven to 400°F (200°C, or gas mark 6).

Heat a deep, oven-safe skillet over medium-high heat and add the avocado oil. Pat the chicken thighs dry and season them with salt and pepper on both sides. Add the chicken thighs to the pan, skin side down, and sear for 5 minutes. You do not need to sear them on the other side; we are just trying to get the skin a little crispy before going into the oven. Remove the thighs from the pan and set them aside.

To make the sauce, add the onion and garlic to the same skillet and sauté for 5 to 7 minutes, until the onion softens. Add the red wine vinegar and simmer for 3 to 5 minutes, or until the vinegar reduces to about half. Add the tomatoes to the pan and stir to combine.

Return the chicken thighs to the pan, skin side up, and nestle them in the sauce; the chicken should not be submerged in the sauce. Tie the bay leaf and rosemary sprig together using kitchen twine and nestle the herb bundle in the sauce.

Transfer the skillet to the oven, uncovered. Cook for 30 to 35 minutes, or until the chicken is cooked through and the skin is crispy.

Remove the skillet from the oven and discard the herb bundle. Taste the sauce and season with salt to taste. Let the chicken rest for 3 to 5 minutes before serving.

INSTANT POT
CHICKEN NOODLE SOUP

SERVES

6

MACROS

Fat: 13.1 g

Carbs: 4.7 g

Net carbs: 3.4 g

Protein: 19.1 g

Fiber: 1.3 g

We have all experienced a few different kinds of chicken noodle soup. From the can to Grandma's noodle soup, this is one meal that just screams feel good! Its soothing and healing properties are undeniable. Personally, I have always used roasted chicken in my chicken noodle soup because it adds more flavor. I am using zucchini noodles, but you can use shirataki noodles instead, if you prefer.

1 tbsp (15 ml) avocado oil

2 tbsp (28 g) butter

1 onion, diced

2 carrots, peeled and sliced

2 ribs celery, diced

4 cloves garlic, minced

1 jalapeño pepper, sliced

1 tsp sea salt, plus more to taste

1 tsp black pepper, plus more to taste

1 tbsp (4 g) chopped fresh parsley, plus more to garnish

1 tbsp (5 g) dried oregano

4 cups (960 ml) Chicken Bone Broth (page 166) or store-bought

2 bone-in, skin-on chicken breasts

4 cups (960 ml) filtered water

1 rosemary sprig

1 bay leaf

2 large zucchinis, spiralized, to serve

Select "sauté" on the Instant Pot. Wait for it to read "hot" and add the avocado oil and butter.

When the butter is melted, add the onion, carrots, celery, garlic and jalapeño to the pan. Sauté the vegetables for 3 to 5 minutes, until the onion is translucent. Season with 1 teaspoon of salt and 1 teaspoon of pepper and add the parsley and oregano. Stir the vegetables and continue to sauté for 1 minute.

Pour the broth over the vegetables and add the chicken breasts. Pour the water over top, then tie the rosemary and bay leaf together using kitchen twine and add it to the pot. Cover the pot and close the steam valve. Select "soup/broth" and set the time for 7 minutes. When the time is up, allow the Instant Pot to go through the natural release cycle, about 10 minutes. You can quick release if you're in a hurry.

Remove the chicken and herb bundle from the pot and shred the chicken using two forks. Discard the skin and herb bundle and save the bones for broth.

Turn the Instant Pot off by selecting "cancel." Return the shredded chicken to the pot and stir to combine. Taste and season with more salt and pepper if necessary.

To serve, put some of the spiralized zucchini noodles on the bottom of a serving dish and add a few ladles of the soup on top. Garnish with fresh parsley.

STOVETOP: Yes, you can certainly make this soup on the stove if you don't have an Instant Pot. Follow all the same steps. You will just have to cook the chicken for about 1 hour instead.

HEARTY KETO
ZUPPA TOSCANA

Zuppa Toscana or "Tuscan Soup" has become a favorite for many of us thanks to Olive Garden. This soup includes many layers of flavors and textures. In this Keto version, we are using cauliflower florets in place of potatoes for a low-carb option. You can also substitute turnips in place of the potatoes.

1 lb (454 g) no-sugar-added spicy Italian sausage (use mild if you are cooking for children)

1 tbsp (14 g) butter

1 onion, diced

2 cloves garlic, minced

Sea salt and black pepper

4 cups (960 ml) Chicken Bone Broth (page 166) or store-bought

1 head cauliflower, cut into florets

1 cup (240 ml) heavy cream

2 handfuls kale leaves

½ tsp xanthan gum (see Note)

Crushed red pepper flakes, to garnish

Add the sausage to a Dutch oven and cook over medium-high heat until it's brown, about 3 to 5 minutes. Remove the sausage from the pan and set it aside.

Add the butter to the pan along with the onion and garlic. Stir and sauté until the onion is tender, about 5 minutes. Season with a couple pinches of salt and pepper.

Pour the broth into the pot and stir to lift up all the brown bits from the bottom of the pan. Add the cauliflower and stir to combine. Bring it to a boil, lower the heat and gently simmer for about 10 minutes to soften the cauliflower.

Return the sausage to the pot along with the heavy cream and kale. Stir and cook for 7 to 10 minutes, until the kale wilts. Turn the heat off and stir in the xanthan gum. As the soup thickens, taste it and season with salt and pepper if necessary.

Garnish with crushed red pepper flakes. The soup will last in the fridge for 1 to 2 days.

NOTE: Xanthan gum is a thickening agent. You can find it in most specialty grocery stores like Whole Foods. But I always grab mine on Amazon. You can use 1 tablespoon (7 g) of coconut flour as a substitution if you have to—but make sure you sift the flour before using it. If you are using coconut flour, add it to the onion and garlic mixture and cook for about 1 minute before adding any of the broth.

CREAMY CHICKEN POTPIE
SOUP

SERVES
6

MACROS
Fat: 16.4 g
Carbs: 10.9 g
Net carbs:
7.2 g
Protein:
19.3 g
Fiber: 3.7 g

No, this isn't Grandma's chicken potpie, but it is a pretty incredible spin on the classic dish. It is very easy to picture yourself with a bowl of this heavenly goodness because it really is that good. All you need are a few staple ingredients you probably already have in your pantry and fridge. In no time, you will have a cozy meal that is a definite crowd-pleaser.

1 lb (454 g) boneless, skinless chicken breasts

4 cups (960 ml) Chicken Bone Broth (page 166) or store-bought, divided

¼ cup (57 g) butter

1 onion, diced

2 ribs celery, diced

2 carrots, peeled and diced

4 cloves garlic, minced

½ tsp sea salt, plus more to taste

½ tsp black pepper

1 tsp Italian seasoning

1 (10-oz [283-g]) bag frozen cut green beans

1 bay leaf

½ cup (120 ml) heavy cream

½ tsp xanthan gum (see Note)

1 tsp fresh parsley, to garnish

Herb-Roasted Delicata Squash (page 169), to serve

Add the chicken breasts to a large pot along with 2 cups (480 ml) of broth. Bring it to a boil, cover the pot and simmer for 15 to 18 minutes. Transfer the chicken and any broth left in the pot to a mixing bowl. Shred the chicken into bite-size pieces and set it aside.

In the same pot you cooked the chicken in, melt the butter over medium-high heat. Add the onion, celery, carrots and garlic to the pot. Sauté the vegetables for about 7 minutes, until they begin to soften. Season with salt, pepper and the Italian seasoning. Add the green beans and continue to sauté for about 2 minutes.

Return the chicken and all of the remaining broth to the pot along with the bay leaf. Stir to lift up all the brown bits from the bottom of the pan and bring it to a rapid boil. Slowly stir in the heavy cream. Continue to simmer the soup over low heat for 7 to 10 minutes.

Turn the heat off and stir in the xanthan gum. As soon as the xanthan gum dissolves, taste and season with salt to taste. Discard the bay leaf and garnish with parsley. Serve with a few pieces of delicata squash on top. Your potpie soup will last in the fridge for 1 to 2 days.

NOTE: Xanthan gum is a thickening agent that can be purchased in most specialty grocery stores. You can also purchase it on Amazon.

MACROS
Fat: 5.1 g
Carbs: 14.5 g
Net carbs:
9.4 g
Protein: 13 g
Fiber: 5.1 g

FEEL-GOOD CABBAGE SOUP

The ultimate feel-good meal! This soup is packed with so many vegetables and nutrients that it can seem a little too good to be true. It is another perfect example of a dump-and-go meal. The most effort you are going to put into making this is prepping the vegetables. It's hearty, healthy and ready in no time. I enjoy adding a can of tuna right on top of the soup when it's almost ready. It adds texture and flavor, but you can certainly leave that out.

2 tbsp (30 ml) avocado oil

1 large onion, chopped

2 carrots, peeled and chopped

2 ribs celery, minced

½ tsp chili powder

Sea salt and black pepper

2 cloves garlic

1 tsp Italian seasoning

4 cups (960 ml) Chicken Bone Broth (page 166) or store-bought

1 cup (240 ml) water

1 small head cabbage, chopped

1 (14.5-oz [411-g]) can fire-roasted diced tomatoes

½ tsp crushed red pepper flakes

1 tbsp (4 g) chopped fresh parsley, plus more to garnish

1 (5-oz [142-g]) can tuna in oil, drained

Heat the avocado oil in a large Dutch oven and add the onion, carrots and celery. Sauté the vegetables for 5 to 7 minutes, until they soften. Season with the chili powder and a couple pinches of salt and pepper.

Add the garlic and Italian seasoning to the pot, stir and sauté for 2 minutes.

Add the broth and water, and bring it to a rapid boil. Add the cabbage and tomatoes, cover and simmer, stirring occasionally, until the cabbage has softened, 35 to 40 minutes.

Stir in the crushed red pepper flakes and 1 tablespoon (4 g) of parsley. Remove the soup from the heat and season with more salt and pepper to taste.

Break up the tuna and add it to the center of the pot of soup. Cover the pot and let it sit for about 5 minutes. The heat from the soup will heat the tuna through. Garnish with more parsley.

EASY BUTTER CHICKEN

I vividly remember the first time I had butter chicken because it felt like a party in my mouth. This dish is on another level of flavor town! The creamy, spiced tomato sauce is definitely the game changer here. Marinating and searing the chicken adds a lot of flavor. But simmering the chicken in the warm spiced-up tomato sauce completely amps up the irresistible factor of this dish.

SERVES
4

MACROS
Fat: 28.4 g
Carbs: 12.6 g
Net carbs: 10.1 g
Protein: 21.2 g
Fiber: 2.5 g

1 lb (454 g) boneless, skinless chicken breasts or thighs, cut into 1-inch (2.5-cm) cubes

¼ cup (60 ml) full-fat Greek yogurt or coconut cream

1 tbsp (6 g) grated ginger

4 cloves garlic, finely minced, divided

2 tsp (3 g) ground turmeric, divided

2 tsp (5 g) ground cumin, divided

1 tsp coriander, divided

3 tsp (7 g) garam masala, divided

1 tsp sea salt, plus more to taste

2 tbsp (30 ml) avocado oil, divided

1 tbsp (14 g) butter

1 onion, finely diced

1 tsp chili powder

1 (14.5-oz [411-g]) can crushed tomatoes

½ cup (120 ml) heavy cream or full-fat coconut milk

Fresh parsley, to garnish

Cauliflower rice (page 154), to serve

Add the chicken, yogurt, ginger, half of the garlic, 1 teaspoon of turmeric, 1 teaspoon of cumin, ½ teaspoon of coriander, 2 teaspoons (5 g) of garam masala and 1 teaspoon of salt to a mixing bowl. Toss all the ingredients to combine and let the chicken marinate for 30 minutes.

Heat a large, deep skillet over medium-high heat and add 1 tablespoon (15 ml) of avocado oil. Divide the chicken into two batches and sear the first batch for 3 minutes on both sides. Remove the chicken from the pan and set it aside. Add the other tablespoon (15 ml) of avocado oil to the pan, sear the rest of the chicken and set it aside.

To make the sauce, lower the heat to medium and add the butter to the same pan along with the onion and remaining garlic. Sauté until the onion is tender, about 5 to 7 minutes. Add the remaining turmeric, cumin, coriander and garam masala and the chili powder to the pan and stir.

Add the tomatoes and scrape the brown bits from the bottom of the pan. Stir in the heavy cream and return the chicken to the sauce. Continue to simmer over low heat for 25 to 30 minutes. Remove the chicken from the heat and serve immediately with fresh parsley and cauliflower rice.

MACROS
Fat: 10.1 g

Carbs: 14.4 g

Net carbs:
10 g

Fiber: 4.4 g

Protein:
25.6 g

HEARTY SUNDAY BEEF CHILI

Chili has become the official food of Sunday night football, right? Or am I just making that up? Well, whatever day of the week you decide to whip up this rich pot of comfort, you are going to love it. As the chili slow cooks, the flavors continue to develop and intensify. The end result is truly a party in your mouth.

4 slices no-sugar-added bacon, diced

1 lb (454 g) ground beef

1 onion, diced

2 carrots, peeled and diced

1 jalapeño pepper, divided, one half diced and one half sliced

4 cloves garlic, finely minced

1 tsp sea salt, plus more to taste

½ tsp black pepper

1½ tsp (2 g) chili powder

1 tsp smoked paprika

1 tsp Italian seasoning

½ tsp ground cumin

1 tbsp (16 g) tomato paste

2 tsp (10 ml) coconut aminos

1 (28-oz [794-g]) can fire-roasted diced tomatoes

2 cups (480 ml) beef broth

1 cup (140 g) diced butternut squash

Avocado pieces, cilantro leaves and diced red onion, to serve

Heat a large Dutch oven over medium-high heat. Add the bacon pieces and cook until crisp, 5 to 7 minutes. Remove the bacon from the pot and set it aside on a plate lined with paper towels.

Leave about 1 tablespoon (15 ml) of bacon fat in the pot and discard the rest. Add the ground beef and cook until brown, about 5 minutes. Stir in the onion, carrots, diced jalapeño, garlic, salt and pepper. Sauté until the vegetables are fork tender, about 7 minutes. Add the chili powder, paprika, Italian seasoning and cumin to the pot. Stir and continue to cook for 3 minutes, then add the tomato paste and coconut aminos. Stir and sauté for 2 minutes to cook the tomato paste.

Add the tomatoes, broth and butternut squash to the pot. Stir to combine and bring the mixture to a boil. Lower the heat to medium-low. Cover the pot and simmer the chili, stirring occasionally, for 1½ to 2 hours or until the chili thickens. When the chili has about 30 minutes left, return the bacon to the pot and stir to combine. Once the chili is done, taste and season with salt.

Serve immediately and top with avocado, cilantro, red onion and the remaining half of the jalapeño.

SUNNY-SIDE UP

I DON'T HAVE TO TELL YOU that breakfast is the most important meal of the day. But, with busy mornings, many of us tend to neglect or just not have time for breakfast. That is exactly why I created recipes such as Mushroom and Leek Frittata (page 132), Low-Carb Breakfast Egg Cups (page 144) and Joyful Matcha Chia Pudding (page 139). These easy make-ahead recipes were created just to make your life a little easier. Prep them at the beginning of the week and have healthy, nutrient-dense breakfasts ready to go for those busy mornings!

And we can't forget about the weekend. Sunday Brunch Salad (page 147), Fancy Avocado Eggs (page 148) and Tex-Mex Good Morning Casserole (page 151) are recipes you just have to make for weekend brunch with friends and family. They are beautiful dishes, and they are definite crowd-pleasers.

MUSHROOM AND LEEK
FRITTATA

Frittatas can be as fancy or simple as you would like them to be. They are one of my favorite ways to clean out my fridge of leftover vegetables and meats. I make a different kind of frittata every week because they are so easy and perfect for meal prep. My mushroom and leek frittata is always a huge hit whenever I make brunch for my friends, and it is going to be a hit at your table.

2 leeks

3 slices no-sugar-added bacon

1 shallot, diced

5 oz (142 g) shiitake mushrooms, sliced

2 cloves garlic, finely minced

¼ tsp sea salt, plus more to taste

¼ tsp black pepper, plus more to taste

6 eggs

2 tbsp (30 ml) heavy cream

2 tbsp (6 g) freshly chopped chives

Preheat the oven to 400°F (200°C, or gas mark 6).

Prepare the leeks by cutting off the dark green ends; discard them or save them for broth. Thinly slice the leeks into rings and discard the root ends. Submerge the leeks in a bowl of cold water and rub gently to remove any dirt. Transfer the leeks to a plate lined with paper towels and set it aside.

Heat a 10-inch (25-cm) cast-iron skillet over medium-high heat and cook the bacon until it's crispy, about 3 to 5 minutes. Remove the bacon from the pan and set it aside.

Add the leeks, shallot, mushrooms and garlic to the pan with the leftover bacon grease. Sauté the vegetables over medium heat until the leeks are tender, about 7 to 10 minutes, and season with ¼ teaspoon of salt and ¼ teaspoon of pepper.

Whisk the eggs and heavy cream together until they are well combined. Season with a pinch of salt and pepper. Pour the egg mixture over the cooked vegetables. Break up the bacon slices into small pieces and scatter them on top of the egg mixture. Scatter the chives on top.

Cook the mixture over medium heat until the edges are set but the center is still runny and loose, about 3 to 5 minutes. Transfer the pan to the oven and bake for 8 to 10 minutes, until the frittata is set.

Let the frittata cool for a few minutes before serving. Leftovers will last in the fridge for up to 3 days.

FOOLPROOF EGG WRAP

SERVES
1

MACROS
Fat: 6.1 g
Carbs: 1.1 g
Net carbs:
1.1 g
Protein: 7.7 g
Fiber: 0 g

Miss breakfast tacos or burritos? Well, look no further because egg wraps are the perfect solution for all my tortilla-loving Keto friends out there. Apart from there being almost zero carbs in these, you can flavor them however you like. Try adding chives or any fresh herbs to the egg before cooking it. The possibilities are endless when it comes to filling them. I usually keep it simple and fill them with sautéed vegetables and ground breakfast sausage. Make it your own and have fun! Note: Macros calculated are for the wraps only.

1 egg

1 tbsp (6 g) Parmesan cheese (optional)

2 oz (57 g) ground breakfast sausage

½ zucchini, diced

1 handful chopped kale leaves

Salt and black pepper, to taste

Sour cream and fresh cilantro leaves, to serve (optional)

Crack the egg in a bowl and whisk until the yolk and the egg white are well incorporated. Whisk the Parmesan cheese (if using) in with the egg and set it aside.

Heat an 8-inch (20-cm) skillet over medium-high heat. Once the pan is hot, spray it with avocado oil spray.

Lower the heat to medium and pour the egg mixture into the hot skillet. Rotate the pan to let the egg spread out in a thin layer. This process is very much like making crepes; the thinner the better.

Once the egg is cooked on one side, about 2 minutes, flip it and cook on the other side, about 1 minute. Remove the egg wrap from the pan and transfer it to a plate to cool.

To serve, cook the breakfast sausage until it is brown, about 5 minutes. Add the zucchini and sauté until it is fork tender. Add the kale and continue to cook until the kale is wilted.

Season with a pinch of salt and pepper if necessary. Fill the egg wraps with the sausage mixture and serve with a dollop of sour cream and fresh cilantro.

PRO TIP: Personally, I would make these fresh every time because they are so easy to make. If you want to prep ahead, I recommend only making enough for 2 days ahead of time.

MACROS

Fat: 20.2 g

Carbs: 14.1 g

Net carbs:
9.8 g

Protein:
16.3 g

Fiber: 4.3 g

ULTIMATE KETO
BREAKFAST HASH

Have you ever fantasized about breakfast the night before or while you sleep? Now I know I am not alone on this one. So, if you've ever had a breakfast fantasy, you were probably dreaming about this hash. Because let me tell you, this is one you just can't go wrong with. The cauliflower soaks up all the flavor of the kielbasa sausage while giving you the body and texture we have all come to love from a potato-based hash.

6 oz (170 g) no-sugar-added kielbasa sausage, sliced

1 tbsp (14 g) butter

1 tbsp (15 ml) avocado oil

½ red bell pepper, cut into ½-inch (1-cm) cubes

½ orange bell pepper, cut into ½-inch (1-cm) cubes

4 oz (113 g) pearl onions, peeled

2 cloves garlic

1 small head cauliflower, cut into ½-inch (1-cm) florets

Sea salt and black pepper

1 tbsp (3 g) finely chopped fresh chives, to garnish

4 eggs (optional)

If you are adding eggs, preheat the oven to 425°F (220°C, or gas mark 7).

Heat a cast-iron pan over medium-high heat and brown the kielbasa sausage, about 3 to 5 minutes. Remove the sausage from the pan and set it aside.

Lower the heat to medium. Add the butter and avocado oil to the pan along with the bell peppers, onions, garlic and cauliflower florets. Sauté the vegetables for 5 to 7 minutes. Season with salt and pepper. Cover the pan and continue to cook the vegetables for 5 to 7 minutes, stirring occasionally, until the cauliflower is tender.

Return the sausage to the pan and stir to combine with the cauliflower mixture. If you aren't adding eggs, garnish with chives and serve.

If you are adding eggs, use a spoon to create four wells. Crack an egg into each well. Sprinkle the chives and a couple pinches of salt and pepper on top and transfer the pan to the oven. Bake until the eggs set and the yolks reach your desired consistency, about 7 minutes. Serve immediately.

JOYFUL MATCHA
CHIA PUDDING

The incredible benefits of chia seeds are undeniable. Add them to smoothies, drinks and desserts for a nutrient-dense snack. Personally, I love chia pudding because the base is a blank canvas and you can add any flavor you like. Matcha powder is my favorite because matcha brings its own array of health benefits and it is very tasty.

SERVES
2

MACROS
Fat: 10.1 g
Carbs: 15.2 g
Net carbs: 5.6 g
Protein: 5.1 g
Fiber: 9.6 g

1 cup (240 ml) unsweetened almond milk, room temperature and divided

1 tsp matcha powder, divided

¼ cup (41 g) chia seeds, divided

Stevia, to taste

Slivered almonds and coconut shavings, to garnish

Divide the almond milk between two ½-pint (240-ml) Mason jars. Add ½ teaspoon of the matcha powder and 2 tablespoons (20 g) of chia seeds to each jar. Add a few drops of stevia into each jar to taste.

Stir all the ingredients together in each jar and attach the lids. Shake the jars for about 1 minute to make sure all the ingredients are well incorporated.

Remove the lid. Let the pudding sit on the countertop for about 5 minutes, or until it starts to settle. Give it a quick stir. Return the lids to the jars and close tightly.

Transfer the jars to the fridge and let the pudding set overnight. The next morning, top the pudding with almonds and coconut shavings.

PRO TIP: Your chia pudding will last in the fridge for up to 1 week, so you can make enough jars to last 1 week.

MACROS

Fat: 4.5 g

Carbs: 1.2 g

Net carbs:
1 g

Protein:
0.2 g

Fiber: 0.2 g

SIMPLE VANILLA
COFFEE CREAMER

If there was one thing I knew I'd have to figure out right away when I decided to transition to the Keto diet, it had to be coffee creamer. I'm not a black coffee kind of girl so this creamer was one of the first things I fell in love with. I will give you options for a completely dairy-free version, but the almond milk and heavy cream combination speaks to my heart in ways I can't describe.

2 cups (480 ml) unsweetened almond milk

½ cup (120 ml) heavy cream or full-fat coconut milk

½ vanilla bean pod or 1 tsp vanilla extract

Stevia or sweetener of your choice, to taste

Pour the almond milk and heavy cream into a 32-ounce (910-ml) Mason jar.

Cut the vanilla bean pod in half lengthwise using a paring knife. Working from one end at a time, hold the tip of the bean against your cutting board and use the dull end of the knife to scrape the vanilla beans out of the pod.

Add the vanilla beans to the Mason jar along with a few drops of stevia to taste. Use a cocktail stirrer to stir the mixture until the vanilla beans are well distributed. Or just put the lid on tightly and shake well to mix.

Store in the fridge for up to a week and a half. Or pour into ice cube trays and freeze for up to 1 month for easy iced coffee drinks.

PRO TIP: If you are the only person in your household that drinks coffee, I recommend cutting the recipe in half for one person. Or you can make the full batch and freeze half of it in ice cube trays.

KETO CREAMER

PUMPKIN-SPICED KETO
GRANOLA

MAKES

8 (32-oz
[907-g])
servings

MACROS

Fat: 22.6 g

Carbs: 6.7 g

Net carbs:
2.3 g

Protein: 8.4 g

Fiber: 4.4 g

Homemade granola is all about patience. You want to bake the granola at a low temperature for a longer period of time to give all the ingredients enough time to develop a golden-brown color and also allow the sweetener to caramelize. You can finally enjoy a bowl of granola with almond milk, or serve it over plain Greek yogurt or Joyful Matcha Chia Pudding (page 139).

¼ cup (61 g) pure pumpkin purée

1 tbsp (14 g) unsalted butter, melted

2 tbsp (24 g) Swerve or monk fruit sweetener

1 egg white

1 tsp vanilla extract

1 tsp pumpkin pie spice

¼ tsp sea salt

1 cup (143 g) raw almonds

½ cup (67 g) raw macadamia nuts (Roasted is fine, just double-check the ingredients if store-brought)

½ cup (69 g) raw pumpkin seeds

¼ cup (40 g) hemp seeds

½ cup (47 g) unsweetened coconut flakes

Preheat the oven to 250°F (120°C). Line a large sheet pan with parchment paper and set it aside.

Place the pumpkin purée, butter, sweetener, egg white, vanilla, pumpkin pie spice and salt in a large bowl. Stir to combine. Set the mixture aside.

Add the almonds and the macadamia nuts to a food processor and pulse until the almonds and macadamia nuts are chopped into small pieces. They should be a little larger than the pumpkin seeds.

Add the almonds, macadamia nuts, pumpkin seeds, hemp seeds and coconut flakes to the bowl with the pumpkin purée mixture. Toss all the ingredients and make sure the nuts and seeds are well coated with pumpkin mixture.

Transfer the granola mixture to the prepared sheet pan and place it in the oven. Roast the granola for 90 minutes, tossing every 30 to 40 minutes, until the granola is crisp and golden brown. If the granola is still wet after 90 minutes, continue to roast it for 15 minutes, or until it's completely dry. Be sure to check it every few minutes to avoid overbaking.

Let the granola cool completely and transfer it to a 32-ounce (910-ml) Mason jar or airtight glass container. When stored in a cool, dry place, your granola will last up to 4 months.

LOW-CARB BREAKFAST
EGG CUPS

Egg muffins are definitely a breakfast favorite because they are easily customizable and can be prepped a few days in advance for an easy breakfast. For all the busy parents, professionals and students out there, this one will be your go-to. There is nothing better than an on-the-go breakfast that is high in protein and low in carbs. It's the perfect start to a busy day.

12 slices no-sugar-added bacon

1 (10-oz [283-g]) package frozen chopped spinach, thawed

12 eggs

½ cup (50 g) grated Parmesan cheese

½ tsp crushed red pepper flakes

Preheat the oven to 400°F (200°C, or gas mark 6).

Cut each bacon strip in half and place both halves in the bottom of each muffin cup of a 12-cup muffin pan. Transfer the pan to the oven and cook the bacon for 15 to 18 minutes. Remove the bacon from the oven, drain the excess fat from the bottom of each muffin cup and set it aside.

Lower the oven temperature to 375°F (190°C, or gas mark 5).

Use your hands to squeeze all the excess liquid from the thawed spinach and put an equal amount of the spinach on top of the bacon in each muffin cup. Crack one egg on top and sprinkle an equal amount of the Parmesan cheese on top of each muffin cup and finish with a pinch of crushed red pepper flakes.

Bake the egg cups for 20 to 25 minutes, or until the egg is set and not jiggling.

Allow the egg cups to cool a little before serving. Store extras in a glass container for up to 4 days in the fridge.

SUNDAY BRUNCH SALAD

SERVES
6

MACROS
Fat: 13.8 g
Carbs: 10 g
Net carbs:
6.5 g
Protein: 5.4 g
Fiber: 3.5 g

Brunch is my favorite part of the weekends. I truly enjoy cooking for my friends and family. One thing I think is a necessary part of a brunch spread is a good salad. This one is a combination of different textures and flavors, and it is a must-make. The simple and easy mustard dressing is the cherry on top and adds an extra layer of flavor.

1 small delicata squash

4 slices no-sugar-added bacon or prosciutto

¼ cup (60 ml) olive oil, plus more if needed

Sea salt and black pepper

2 tbsp (30 ml) lemon juice

1 tbsp (15 ml) spicy brown mustard

1 clove garlic, finely minced

½ tsp monk fruit golden sweetener

1 (5-oz [142-g]) package mixed greens or spinach

1 handful chopped dinosaur kale leaves

1 avocado, sliced

Bagel seasoning, to serve (The Trader Joe's or Balanced Bites brands are wonderful.)

Preheat the oven to 400°F (200°C, or gas mark 6).

Wash and scrub the squash thoroughly and cut off the ends. Cut the squash in half lengthwise and remove the seeds. Then cut them into ¼-inch (6-mm) half-moon slices and set the squash aside.

Place the bacon on a large sheet pan. Transfer the pan to the oven and cook for 15 to 18 minutes, until the bacon is crisp. Remove the bacon from the pan and set it aside on a plate lined with paper towels.

Discard half of the bacon fat from the sheet pan and add the squash to the same pan. Note that if you are using prosciutto, you need to add about 2 tablespoons (30 ml) of olive oil to the squash, because the prosciutto does not give off much fat when cooked. Season with a couple of pinches of salt and pepper and toss to coat. Transfer the squash to the oven and roast it for 25 to 30 minutes, flipping halfway through until the squash is golden brown and crispy on the outside. Remove the pan from the oven and set the squash aside to cool slightly.

In the meantime, make the dressing. Add the lemon juice, mustard, garlic and sweetener to a small bowl. Stir to combine. Slowly whisk ¼ cup (60 ml) of olive oil in with the rest of the ingredients until it is well incorporated.

Put the mixed greens and kale in a large serving bowl and add the dressing to the greens. Toss to combine.

To serve, add the slightly cooled squash on top of the greens, crumble the bacon over top and finish with avocado slices. Sprinkle bagel seasoning on the avocado slices.

SERVES
4

MACROS
Fat: 20.1 g
Carbs: 6.3 g
Net carbs:
1.8 g
Protein:
8.6 g
Fiber: 4.5 g

FANCY AVOCADO EGGS

These are beautiful to look at and they're incredibly scrumptious. This is another brunch favorite that combines all the healthy fats of an avocado with the subtle earthy flavor of eggs. When it comes to toppings for this beauty of a dish, the possibilities are endless.

2 ripe avocados

4 eggs

1 tbsp (15 ml) olive oil

Sea salt and black pepper

Goat cheese, fresh cilantro leaves and fresh chives, to serve

Preheat the oven to 425°F (220°C, or gas mark 7).

Cut the avocados in half and remove the pits. Scoop out enough of the avocado flesh to create a well for the eggs. Place the avocado halves on a sheet pan. Crack an egg inside of each avocado half, drizzle with the olive oil and sprinkle with a pinch of salt and pepper.

Bake the avocados in the oven for 12 to 15 minutes, or until the yolk reaches your desired consistency.

Serve with a sprinkling of goat cheese, cilantro and chives. Store any leftovers in the fridge for 2 days. It's best to reheat them in the oven or toaster oven.

PRO TIP: To add some variety, or if you are not a fan of goat cheese and cilantro, you can absolutely make this your own and add your favorite toppings. Some options include bacon, other cheeses, tomatoes, kale or spinach. Add these toppings after you crack the egg in the avocado, then transfer them to the oven.

TEX-MEX GOOD MORNING
CASSEROLE

SERVES
6

MACROS
Fat: 29.5 g
Carbs: 5.3 g
Net carbs: 4.5 g
Protein: 33.5 g
Fiber: 0.8 g

Casseroles are always very appealing because they make for easy prep-ahead meals. You can simply layer your casserole the night before and then bake it the next day or when you are ready to serve. This one includes all the fixings. It's packed with vegetables, eggs and ground meat. It's also perfect for meal prep because you can make this ahead of time, cut it into squares, store it in the fridge and have a quick breakfast ready to go.

1 lb (454 g) ground beef

1 onion, diced

1 bell pepper, diced

2 cloves garlic, finely minced

1 tsp taco seasoning

1 tsp sea salt, plus a pinch more

1 tsp black pepper, plus a pinch more

½ cup (120 ml) sour cream, room temperature

2 tbsp (6 g) chives, divided

12 eggs, room temperature

1 cup (113 g) grated Cheddar cheese

Avocado slices, to serve

Preheat the oven to 350°F (175°C, or gas mark 4).

Heat a large oven-safe skillet over medium-high heat and brown the ground beef until it is no longer pink, about 5 to 7 minutes. Drain most of the fat from the beef. Add the onion, bell pepper and garlic to the pan with the beef and continue to sauté until the pepper is tender. Add the taco seasoning, salt and pepper. Stir to combine. Add the sour cream, half of the chives and the eggs to a bowl and whisk to combine. Season with a pinch of salt and pepper.

Remove the pan from heat and set aside half the ground beef mixture, leaving the other half of the ground beef mixture in the pan. Pour half of the egg mixture into the bottom of the pan and top with the remaining ground beef mixture. Then pour the remaining egg mixture into the pan and sprinkle the Cheddar cheese over top.

At this point, if you are prepping ahead of time, cover the casserole with aluminum foil and transfer the casserole to the fridge for a maximum of overnight and bake when you are ready.

If you are cooking immediately, transfer the casserole to the oven and bake for 35 to 40 minutes, or until the egg mixture is firm and the cheese is golden and bubbly.

Allow the casserole to cool for 10 minutes. Cut the casserole into squares and serve with avocado slices or store in an airtight glass container. The casserole will keep in the fridge for up to 1 week.

BACK TO
BASICS

I WANT YOU TO FEEL AS CONFIDENT AS POSSIBLE IN YOUR KITCHEN. So, this chapter is filled with all the necessities I think you will need to make the very best of your Keto experience. From easy side dishes to necessary staples such as Chicken Bone Broth (page 166), these recipes were created especially to be your wingmen when it comes to dinnertime.

The side dishes I've included in this chapter are all very complementary to the rest of the recipes in the book. No-Fuss Fluffy Cauliflower Rice (page 154) and Easy Garlic Broccolini (page 157) are just a couple of examples of side dishes that are incredibly universal and can be served alongside almost any main dish.

I'm also sharing my recipes for arrabbiata sauce (page 162) and The Best Homemade Harissa Sauce (page 170). Arrabbiata is not very different from marinara sauce; it's just spicy. It adds an immense amount of flavor to any dish where you would normally use marinara sauce. You will notice I use harissa as a flavor booster in a lot of my recipes. You can find harissa sauce in most stores and online, but there is nothing better than homemade harissa.

SERVES
2

MACROS
Fat: 7 g
Carbs: 8 g
Net carbs: 4 g
Protein: 4 g
Fiber: 4 g

NO-FUSS FLUFFY
CAULIFLOWER RICE

Cauliflower is one of the healthiest cruciferous vegetables out there. It's loaded with fiber, vitamins and potassium. So, it is the perfect substitution for rice on the Keto diet. The number one question I get when it comes to cauliflower rice is, "How do I make my cauliflower rice fluffy and not mushy"? Well, this step-by-step recipe includes my foolproof method for achieving always-perfect cauliflower rice.

1 tbsp (15 ml) avocado oil
1 (12-oz [340-g]) bag cauliflower rice

Garlic seasoning of choice

Heat the avocado oil in a skillet over high heat and add the cauliflower. Cook the cauliflower, stirring continuously, for 3 to 5 minutes, until it is tender and fluffy.

Keep the temperature on high for the entire cooking process while continuously tossing the cauliflower rice. This will help get rid of all the excess liquid very quickly while allowing the cauliflower rice to keep its shape.

Season the rice with your favorite garlic seasoning. Waiting until the rice is cooked to season is an extra effort to ensure your cauliflower rice is not mushy. Adding salt or salt-based seasonings to any vegetable like cauliflower only draws out liquid from the vegetables.

Transfer the cauliflower rice to a serving bowl.

EASY GARLIC BROCCOLINI

SERVES
4

MACROS
Fat: 6.3 g
Carbs: 8.5 g
Net carbs:
7.2 g
Protein: 4 g
Fiber: 1.3 g

Broccolini or "baby broccoli" is simply the more delicate version of broccoli. It's slightly sweeter and is similar to asparagus in flavor. When I cook this marvelous vegetable, I like to make sure I am adding other components that will only enhance the earthy flavor of the broccolini. And that's exactly why this is my go-to way to cook broccolini. I simply sauté it in olive oil and butter with lots of garlic—and that is all she wrote.

2 bunches broccolini

1 tbsp (15 ml) olive oil

1 tbsp (14 g) butter

4 cloves garlic, finely minced

Sea salt and black pepper

Bring a large pot with about 8 cups (1.9 L) of water to a boil and season with a generous amount of sea salt. Remove and discard the bottom third of the broccolini stems. If you have some that are very thick, cut them in half lengthwise.

While the water comes to a boil, prepare an ice bath of half ice and half cold water. When the water comes to a full boil, add the trimmed broccolini and cook for 2 to 3 minutes, until the broccolini stalks are crisp and tender.

Remove the broccolini from the boiling water and immediately transfer it to the ice bath to stop the cooking process. Drain in a colander and set the broccolini aside.

Heat the olive oil and butter in a large skillet and add the garlic. Sauté for about 1 minute, until the garlic is fragrant. Add the broccolini, toss and sauté to heat the broccolini through, about 2 minutes. Season with a few pinches of salt and pepper.

SERVES
4

MACROS
Fat: 3.3 g
Carbs: 7.8 g
Net carbs:
4.7 g
Protein:
2.9 g
Fiber: 3.1 g

ALWAYS PERFECT
CAULIFLOWER MASH

Who needs mashed potatoes when you can have vegetable mash that is just as heavenly? All it takes is a few easy steps to achieve rich, creamy and nutty cauliflower mash. The buttery, garlic flavor of this cauliflower mash is the perfect side for many dishes. I especially love it served with Braised Mushroom Short Ribs (page 92).

---

1 head cauliflower, cut into florets

1 tbsp (14 g) butter

2 cloves garlic, roughly chopped

1 tsp fresh rosemary

Sea salt and black pepper

Place a steamer insert into a saucepan and fill the pan with water to just below the bottom of the steamer.

Bring the water to a boil, add the cauliflower, cover and steam until the cauliflower is fork tender, about 10 minutes.

Meanwhile, melt the butter in a small saucepan and add the garlic and rosemary. Sauté for about 1 minute, until the garlic is fragrant. Remove the pan from the heat and set it aside.

Transfer the cauliflower to a food processor and pulse on high until it's almost smooth. Pour the butter mixture over the cauliflower. Season with salt and pepper to taste. Continue to blend the mixture until it's well combined and smooth.

PRO TIP: The possibilities are endless when it comes to how you can flavor your cauliflower mash. Try using other herbs, such as thyme and oregano, instead of rosemary. You can also add sour cream, cream cheese or Parmesan cheese.

FOOLPROOF ZUCCHINI
NOODLES

SERVES
2

MACROS
Fat: 14.1 g

Carbs: 6.1 g

Net carbs:
4.1 g

Protein: 2.4 g

Fiber: 2 g

There are several different substitutions for pasta or noodles when it comes to choosing a healthier option. Zucchini noodles are definitely the most popular choice for a low-carb swap. Although incredibly versatile and easy to make, there are a few essential steps you need to take to ensure you always end up with the best noodles that will complement any dish.

2 large zucchinis

½ tsp sea salt

2 tbsp (30 ml) olive or avocado oil

Use a spiralizer to spiralize the zucchinis.

Place the noodles in a large bowl lined with cheesecloth and sprinkle with the sea salt. Let the noodles sit for about 15 minutes, then wrap the cheesecloth around the noodles and squeeze out all the excess liquid.

Heat the olive or avocado oil in a nonstick skillet. Sauté the noodles, tossing frequently, for 3 to 5 minutes over medium-high heat to heat the zucchini through. Serve immediately.

NOTE: I love the Inspiralized brand spiralizer. It is the best spiralizer on the market in my opinion. You always want to start with great tools to assist you in your kitchen. Better tools lead to better results.

MACROS

Fat: 7.5 g

Carbs: 10.6 g

Net carbs:
9.8 g

Protein: 3.1 g

Fiber: 0.8 g

CHARLOTTE'S ARRABBIATA

I do love a good tomato sauce. It's so versatile, and you can have so much fun creating a lot of different meals. I have to admit that arrabbiata sauce is hands down the one sauce I think everyone should have in their kitchen at all times! The only real difference between arrabbiata and your classic marinara is that arrabbiata is spicy. We simply add crushed red pepper flakes to make arrabbiata "angry" sauce. Of course, if you aren't a fan of a spicy sauce, you can just omit the crushed red pepper flakes and follow the rest of this recipe to make a classic marinara sauce.

¼ cup (60 ml) olive oil

2 tbsp (7 g) crushed red pepper flakes

1 onion, diced

4 cloves garlic, finely minced

1 tsp sea salt, divided

2 (28-oz [794-g]) cans crushed tomatoes

8 basil leaves, chopped

½ tsp black pepper

Heat the olive oil in a large Dutch oven over medium-high heat and add the crushed red pepper flakes. Sauté the pepper flakes, stirring frequently, for 2 to 3 minutes. Skip this step if you want to make classic marinara.

Add the onion and garlic to the pot and season with ½ teaspoon of salt. Cook the onion and garlic for 5 to 7 minutes, stirring frequently, until the onion is translucent.

Add the tomatoes to the pan and stir thoroughly. Lower the heat to medium and simmer the sauce for 25 minutes while stirring occasionally. If you have larger chunks of tomatoes, break them up as the sauce cooks.

After 25 minutes, add the basil leaves, the remaining ½ teaspoon of salt and black pepper to the sauce. Continue to simmer the sauce over low heat for 5 to 7 minutes.

Let the sauce cool and transfer it to clean Mason jars for storage in the fridge for up to 4 days. For a longer shelf life, freeze the sauce in freezer-friendly containers or ziplock bags for up to 6 months.

COZY BOLOGNESE SAUCE

Bolognese is just a fancy way of saying "meat sauce." Although it is commonly served over pasta, this sauce is incredibly versatile. When you have leftover Bolognese in the fridge, the possibilities are endless. You can stuff peppers, wrap it in egg wraps (page 135) with fresh greens or make mini lasagna muffins—and so much more!

SERVES

6

MACROS

Fat: 26.3 g

Carbs: 14 g

Net carbs: 13 g

Protein: 18.5 g

Fiber: 1 g

1 lb (454 g) ground beef

2 tbsp (30 ml) olive oil

1 onion, diced

2 carrots, peeled and diced

4 cloves garlic, finely minced

1 tsp sea salt, plus more to taste

1 tsp Italian seasoning

½ tsp crushed red pepper flakes

¼ cup (66 g) tomato paste

2 tbsp (30 ml) coconut aminos

1 (28-oz [794-g]) can crushed tomatoes

1 cup (240 ml) heavy cream

6 basil leaves, chopped

Crumble the ground beef into a large Dutch oven and brown the meat over medium-high heat for about 5 minutes. I like to use a potato masher to break up the beef while it cooks. Drain the meat and discard the fat.

Add the olive oil, onion, carrots and garlic to the pot with the meat and sauté for 5 to 7 minutes, or until the onion is tender and the carrots are al dente or almost cooked through. Add the salt, Italian seasoning and crushed red pepper flakes to the meat and vegetables. Stir to combine. Stir in the tomato paste and coconut aminos, and cook for about 1 to 2 minutes.

Pour the tomatoes into the pot and stir to lift up all the brown bits from the bottom of the pan.

Bring the sauce to a slow simmer and stir in the heavy cream and basil. Lower the heat to medium-low, cover the pot and continue to simmer for 2 hours, stirring occasionally.

Uncover the sauce and season with more salt if necessary. Continue to simmer the sauce, uncovered, for 3 to 5 minutes. Remove the sauce from the heat and serve hot.

PRO TIP: You can freeze the leftover Bolognese for up to 4 months. So, make a double batch so you can have meat sauce on hand for a long time.

CHICKEN BONE BROTH

MAKES
8 cups
(1.9 L)

MACROS
Fat: 13.3 g
Carbs: 4.8 g
Net carbs:
3.7 g
Protein:
30.6 g
Fiber: 1.1 g

Although there are many wonderful options on the market for clean and flavorful broth, there is still nothing better than making your own broth at home. Because I like to use roasted chicken bones for my broth, I always save my bones from other recipes in the freezer until I'm ready to make broth. You will also notice I add chicken feet to my broth. It adds rich flavor and nutrients such as collagen, vitamins and lots of minerals.

2 lbs (907 g) chicken bones from 2 roasted chicken

4 chicken feet

16 cups (3.8 L) filtered water

1 tbsp (15 ml) apple cider vinegar

1 tsp sea salt

1 tsp peppercorns

1 onion, quartered

3 carrots, peeled and halved

2 ribs celery with leaves attached, cut into thirds

4 cloves garlic, peeled and halved

1 bay leaf

½ bunch fresh parsley

Place the bones and chicken feet in a large stockpot and add the water, vinegar, salt and peppercorns. Bring it to a boil and reduce to simmer. At this time, you want to skim off any impurities that float to the surface. Cover the pot and continue to simmer over low heat for 6 hours.

Add the onion, carrots, celery, garlic, bay leaf and parsley to the pot. Continue to cook the broth on a low simmer for 9 hours. Be careful not to bring it to a rapid boil.

Strain the broth through a fine-mesh strainer and discard the solids. Cool the strained broth to room temperature and refrigerate overnight. The next day, skim off the fat from the top and continue to store in the fridge for 3 to 5 days. For a longer shelf life, transfer the broth to freezer-friendly containers and freeze for up to 3 months.

INSTANT POT: Put the chicken bones and chicken feet in a 6-quart (5.7-L) Instant Pot. Add the onion, celery, carrots, apple cider vinegar, salt, peppercorns, garlic, bay leaf and parsley to the Instant Pot. Add 10 to 11 cups (2.4 to 2.6 L) of filtered water, cover the Instant Pot and close the sealing valve. Select "soup/broth" and set the time to 2 hours. When it's done, let it naturally release for 30 minutes. Follow the instructions above for straining and storing the broth.

SLOW COOKER: Add the bones and chicken feet to the slow cooker. Pour in 12 cups (2.9 L) of hot water along with apple cider vinegar, salt and peppercorns. Cook on low for 6 hours, then add the onion, carrots, celery, garlic, bay leaf and parsley. Continue to cook on low for 9 hours. Follow the instructions above for straining and storing.

HERB-ROASTED
DELICATA SQUASH

SERVES
4

MACROS
Fat: 6.3 g
Carbs: 2.7 g
Net carbs: 2.1 g
Protein: 0.6 g
Fiber: 0.6 g

Before eating Keto, I had never had delicata squash. But now, I can't go a week without it. It's a little sweet, and when you pair it with herbs and a nutty fat such as butter, it just gets better and better. This makes a wonderful side dish, but I love serving it with a bowl of Creamy Chicken Potpie Soup (page 123).

1 medium or 2 small delicata squash

1 tbsp (15 ml) olive oil

1 tbsp (14 g) butter, melted

Sea salt and black pepper

1 tsp dried thyme

Preheat the oven to 425°F (220°C, or gas mark 7).

Wash the squash and give it a good scrub with a produce brush. Cut the squash in half lengthwise and scoop out the seeds. Cut each squash half into ¼-inch (6-mm) half-moon slices and transfer them to a large sheet pan lined with parchment paper.

Drizzle the olive oil and butter over the squash and sprinkle with a couple pinches of salt and pepper and the dried thyme. Toss to make sure the squash is well coated and spread out the pieces in a single layer.

Roast the squash in the preheated oven for 15 minutes. Flip it and roast it for 10 to 15 minutes.

Serve immediately. Store leftovers in an airtight container for up to 5 days. Reheat in the oven or toaster oven.

MACROS
Fat: 6.5 g
Carbs: 6.5 g
Net carbs:
4.8 g
Protein: 2.2 g
Fiber: 1.7 g

THE BEST HOMEMADE
HARISSA SAUCE

Harissa is an ingredient that is always in my kitchen, and I use it in a lot of my recipes. I know a lot of people either have a hard time finding harissa or they don't know how to make it at home. So, I'm here to hook you up with my homemade harissa recipe. Harissa is actually very simple and easy; the essential ingredients are the dried chilis. Everything else you most likely already have in your pantry.

4 dried chilis de Arbol (add more if you want it spicier)

5 dried California or New Mexico chilis (these are milder)

1 red bell pepper, deseeded and cut in half

1 tsp coriander seeds

1 tsp crushed red pepper flakes

1 tsp cumin seeds

1 tsp fennel seeds

7½ oz (213 g) fire-roasted diced tomatoes

5 cloves garlic

1 tbsp (16 g) tomato paste

1 tsp smoked paprika

2 tbsp (30 ml) lemon juice

¼ cup (60 ml) olive oil

1 tsp sea salt, plus more to taste

½ tsp black pepper, plus more to taste

Preheat the oven's broiler to high. Set the oven rack about 6 inches (15 cm) away from the heat source.

Place all the dried chilis in a deep mixing bowl and cover with hot water. Once the chilis are submerged, cover the bowl and let it steam for about 15 minutes. Once the chilis are rehydrated, drain them and remove the stems and seeds. Transfer them to a food processor, but do not process yet. Set aside.

Line a sheet pan with foil and place the bell pepper on the sheet pan cut side down. Cook the pepper under the broiler for 5 to 8 minutes, or until the pepper halves have blackened and blistered. Put the blackened pepper in a bowl and cover tightly. Let the pepper steam as it cools, about 20 minutes. Remove and discard the skin. Place the pepper in the food processor and set it aside.

Add the coriander, pepper flakes, cumin and fennel seeds to the food processor along with the tomatoes, garlic, tomato paste, paprika, lemon juice, olive oil, salt and pepper. Blend all the ingredients together, scraping down the sides of the food processor as needed, until the mixture is smooth. Taste the mixture and adjust the seasoning to taste. Add more paprika for smokiness, lemon for acidity or salt to taste. Season with more pepper if necessary.

ACKNOWLEDGMENTS

To Uncle Everett, the one person who seems to always make the world a better place. Thank you for being my biggest fan, taste tester and the most incredible father figure in my life. The pure kindness you continue to show me means more to me than you will ever know. Thank you for the uncontrollable laughs and most of all, thank you for always loving me.

Mama, I know you are with me always. Thank you for being my forever angel. Thank you for being my Mother. I love you so much and I am forever grateful for the life lessons you taught me at a young age. I am forever your daughter.

Sissy! Can you believe I did this? Thank you for keeping me sane, sis. I am so grateful for every moment of growth our relationship has had. You are my sister, but we have chosen to be best friends—and I always know you have my back. Thank you for keeping me company and making me laugh on those days when I didn't think I could write this book. I love you, Caroline. Can't wait to celebrate!

To Ellen Moore, Miracle and Ricky! I love you to the moon, baby! I am so proud to be your sister, and I hope I'm doing it right. Thank you for believing in me and always making me smile.

To Takeyah and over a decade of hugs, cries, laughter (a lot of laughter), love and forever friendship. The fact that we can go months without seeing each other but come together like no time has passed is one of the greatest joys of my life. Thank you for being my best friend. Here's to another decade, boo.

To one of my greatest inspirations, Diane Sanfilippo. You have become more than just a mentor and someone I truly look up to. You have become a dear friend and I am so grateful. You are always striving to give everyone an opportunity to be great. And I am so blessed to be one of those people.

To the beautiful people who have made this African girl's dream come true. My Page Street family! Madeline, Meg and everyone who has been so incredibly kind, patient, helpful and insightful. I appreciate you. I adore you! Thank you so much for giving me the opportunity to make my mark.

To my fellow bloggers, entrepreneurs, foodies and all-around phenomenal women who are running the world, thank you for your part in building and strengthening our community. Thank you for inspiring, teaching, learning, creating and giving the immense amount of hard work and dedication you put in every day.

To all of you who have purchased this book, I don't even know how to express my gratitude. This is truly a labor of love from my kitchen to yours. I hope you feel the love and care that went into these recipes, and I hope you and your family enjoy many fun and flavor-filled meals with *One-Pot Keto Cooking* by your side.

And last but certainly never least, to my Clean Foodie Cravings readers, subscribers and internet family! You know how much I adore each and every one of you. Without your support, I would have never dreamed I would be living my dreams. I see each and every one of you! I am forever grateful, and I will continue to strive for the best for our community. You are and will forever be my people!

ABOUT THE AUTHOR

Charlotte Smythe is the creator, writer and foodie behind the successful blog Clean Foodie Cravings. She started her blog because she enjoys learning and growing in the kitchen. But through her eagerness to clean up her own lifestyle, her website blossomed into a community of people who are simply trying to live their best life.

Charlotte takes pride in creating an abundance of recipes that cater to a wide range of people and lifestyle choices—although the Keto diet is her first love. It is also very important to her that she continues to strive to make sure anyone who visits her little corner of the internet is able to find a recipe that speaks to their lifestyle, wants and needs.

Through hard work comes a little recognition. Charlotte's recipes and writing have been featured by *Paleo Magazine*, *Country Living*, Whole30.com, thefeedfeed.com and many more.

If she's not in her kitchen cooking up something scrumptious, she enjoys yoga, watching and learning from her favorite foodies, cheering on her favorite basketball team and hitting up all her favorite sushi spots in Minneapolis, Minnesota, where she calls home.

INDEX